# Pilates
## Three in One

HINKLER
BOOKS

First published in 2006
by Hinkler Books Pty Ltd
17-23 Redwood Drive
Dingley, VIC 3172, Australia
www.hinklerbooks.com

Printed and bound in China

ISBN 1 7415 7413 7

When practising Pilates, always do the warm up exercises before attempting
any individual postures. It is recommended that you check with your doctor
or healthcare professional before commencing any exercise regime. Whilst
every care has been taken in the preparation of this material, the Publishers
and their respective employees or agents will not accept responsibility for
injury or damage occasioned to any person as a result of participation in
the activities described in this book.

# S I M P L Y

# PILATES

Editors: Bridget Blair & Robyn Sheahan-Bright
Creative Director: Sam Grimmer
Photography: Peter Wakeman
Design: Sam Grimmer

# CONTENTS

# INTRODUCTION

The Pilates Method of exercising has become one of the most sought-after ways of maintaining one's fitness. Unique in its approach to working the body 'smart', not 'hard', it is renowned for achieving long-term physical benefits. It is endorsed by medical and fitness professionals in many countries for its ability to re-educate the body to move efficiently, improving the quality of an individual's daily activities.

Originally developed by German-born Joseph Pilates in the early 1900s, the technique has evolved, taking on various forms. During World War I, Pilates used his knowledge of strengthening the body to rehabilitate injured soldiers. He later operated his own exercise studio in New York, where many dancers, athletes and actresses were attracted to his training methods as a way to maintain a strong, supple and streamlined physique. Pilates called his method 'The Art of Contrology', though over the years it has taken on his own name of 'Pilates'. Its essential concept is to stretch and strengthen the body with heed to symmetry and alignment.

His movement system was designed to deliver the ultimate full-body workout in a gentle and effective manner, borrowing principles from various Eastern and Western exercise philosophies. He believed, foremost, that the mind controls the muscles and that endless repetitions of meaningless exercises do more harm than good. When exercising using Pilates' principles, the outcome is better posture, stronger and more flexible muscles, greater energy and an increased ability to cope with day-to-day stresses.

Pilates has become very popular with people in high-profile professions, such as dancers and actors, and has therefore become extremely 'trendy'. However, it is not, like some other exercise regimes, destined to become a transitory fad, since it is a highly disciplined form of exercise with a record of proven results.

# THE BENEFITS

A commitment to the Pilates mat work will promote greater trunk and pelvic stability, as well as improving movement and muscle control of and around the spine itself. Such control is requisite to both preventing spinal injury, and managing any existing back or neck pain. Pilates exercises specifically aim to create muscle balance in the body, greater coordination of movement and control of the abdominals and breathing. These exercises encourage the use of the body as a whole unit, developing strong, lean musculature, rather than allowing individual muscle groups to develop isolated strength and to become bulky. The philosophies behind the Pilates Method have been constant for many years, but it is only recently that people have begun to recognise its 'tried-and-true', more holistic approach to maintaining physical fitness.

The Pilates repertoire of exercises is very adaptable, with most exercises having both a modified and a progressive version. This is why Pilates can enable people of all fitness levels to enjoy its benefits. A typical Pilates mat work session will progress the exercises in a particular order, so that the muscles are prepared for subsequent exercises and a full-body workout is achieved. When these series of movements are executed in a precise and flowing manner, an authentic synergy between mind and body is met, natural poise is achieved, and overall well-being is enhanced.

*Simply Pilates* is a compilation of beginner-level exercises based on Joseph Pilates' original body-conditioning concepts. The sequence is designed to be easily interpreted for you to establish and maintain postural strength and balance. The Pilates way of exercising involves starting from basic awareness of your posture, movement and breathing. Once these essential concepts are embodied, you will find its benefits will translate to your everyday activities. Pilates will add to your enjoyment of life and assist you in reaching your fitness potential.

# PRACTICAL MATTERS

When exercising the Pilates way, ensure that you are aware of the need to flatten your abdominals to stabilise your pelvis and lower back. If you have a history of injury, or physical limitation, or if you are pregnant, it is recommended that you consult your physician before embarking on any exercise program in order to assess the suitability of various movements for your body. Once you have received the all-clear, regular practice will help you to achieve your fitness goals more quickly, and will assist in the maintenance of optimum body balance. Three to four times a week is fine. Adapt the step-by-step directions to suit your physical capabilities and fitness level. The Pilates mat work is designed to allow you to proceed through the exercises at your own pace. Build up to the entire exercise program gradually, adding repetitions as you get stronger—though remember that 'less is more' and a maximum of 6–10 repetitions for each exercise is sufficient, providing each execution is of good quality.

## REQUIREMENTS

You will need certain materials in order to do your Pilates mat work. The mat or carpet surface which you select must offer you some comfort, but must not be so soft that your body sinks into it and the natural curvature of your spine loses integrity. You will need a small pillow and a towel to assist with some exercises and stretches. You may also rest your head on either of these during the mat work if you need neck support. Finally, it is recommended that you use a low chair or box to relieve lower back tension during some sitting exercises.

# PILATES PRINCIPLES

There are six principles which help to define the purpose of the Pilates Method:

## CONCENTRATION

The mind wills the body to perform. It is said that without mental focus during a workout, essentially only half a workout is being done. Visualisation assists the individual in using the correct muscles.

## CONTROL

Pilates exercises require absolute muscle control to both guard against injury and to achieve full functional benefit from each movement.

## CENTRE

The abdomen, lower back, hips and buttocks comprise our 'centre', the region which Joseph referred to as our 'powerhouse'—all energy for movement begins here, then continues to the extremities.

## FLUIDITY

It is intended that the exercises be executed with optimal flow and grace. There are no static or isolated movements, and manoeuvres are never rushed.

## PRECISION

Each movement has purpose and each repetition of an exercise is of high quality, so favourable muscle patterning will become second nature.

## BREATH

Breathing with intention assists with muscle control. Inhaling and exhaling fully promotes purification and oxygenation of the lungs and bloodstream which energises the system and gives a feeling of well-being.

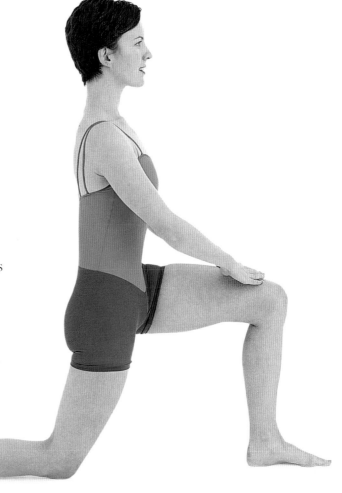

# CENTRING & BREATHING

*Each time you begin the Pilates mat work, be aware of the following important concepts, as they are fundamental in executing the exercises in their correct and intended form.*

## NEUTRAL PELVIS

The pelvis is the junction between the torso and legs, to which various muscles attach for movement and stabilising purposes. When the pelvis tilts forward or backward the curve of the lower back will change. Current spinal health research indicates that the natural curves of the spine should be maintained during exercise in order to strengthen the muscles essential to postural support. The correct positioning of the pelvis is crucial to maintaining this natural spinal shape. 'Neutral Pelvis' is achieved when the pelvic bones tilt neither way, but simply rest where hip and back muscles can remain fairly relaxed. The easiest way of finding this position is to recognise that your pubic bone and hip bones (iliac crests) all form a parallel level with the floor when lying on your back. (These bones should be aligned in the same plane when the body is in any position.) Neutral Pelvis is the ideal position in which to strengthen the deep abdominals.

## CORRECT ABDOMINALS

Strong abdominals are more important to you than achieving a 'six-pack'. Good quality movement while preventing spinal injury begins by working the muscles from the inside out. This means refining the action of the abdominal muscles so that you can work the deeper layers responsible for maintaining 'core' stability. To target this area you need to focus on the 'drawing in and up' of the lower abdomen—between the pubic bone and navel. Imagine zipping up the abdominals starting from the pubic bone, as if you're zipping up tight jeans! Use pelvic floor muscles and flatten and tighten the abdominals towards the floor, without actually disturbing your Neutral Pelvis. Try not to tense up the gluteal muscles (buttocks). Imagine that your whole navel and waist area is shrinking, as though held in by a corset. During a Pilates session an instructor would

typically describe this action as 'scooping', 'drawing in' or 'pressing the navel to spine' in order to ensure that the deeper layers of abdominals are strengthened.

## BREATH CONTROL

Various breathing techniques are used for different purposes. Many people breathe insufficiently in order to nourish, energise and detoxify the body. Focusing on regular breathing when exercising is important, as oxygen is needed to assist in physical stamina, and breath monitoring helps to assist muscle use or relaxation. Breathe in through the nose and out through the mouth. Keep a steady pace, and ensure both the lower abdominals and the corset action of the waist remain active. When learning the Pilates Method of body conditioning, abdominal strength and control is a primary focus. Lateral, or sideways, breathing is taught so that the abdominal focus can remain strong. This is achieved when the side and back of the ribcage expand during inhalation and with each exhalation the abdominals 'scooping in and upward' is re-emphasised.

## PREPARATORY NOTE

These posture cues are the basis of the Pilates Method. This specific attention to detail is imperative to both encourage correct use of muscles and to enable the release of muscles that have become overworked. Once this basis of functional posture is established, the Pilates exercises can be practised with a deeper understanding of restoring balance to the body. Attention must be paid to alignment of the body as a whole—from head to toes. To prepare for each exercise, the Neutral Pelvis Position should be established and the natural curves of the spine maintained, while ensuring the hip, knee and ankle joints are in line. The easiest way to align the legs is to place the heels opposite the 'sitting bones', which are the lowest bony protrusions of the pelvis that you may be aware of when sitting on a hard surface. Over time, constant awareness of good posture and muscular support will increase the endurance of the body's 'core' muscles. This will assist in the release of unnecessary tension and the management of aches and pains.

# BREATHING EXERCISE

***Purpose*** *To establish the basic postural concepts: maintaining a Neutral Pelvis Position while developing the coordination of lateral breathing with correct abdominal use. This technique of breathing and abdominal control is essentially how we begin every exercise. With practice it will gradually become second nature. Getting this correct will enable you to progress through the Pilates mat work and will challenge your strength, control and endurance.*

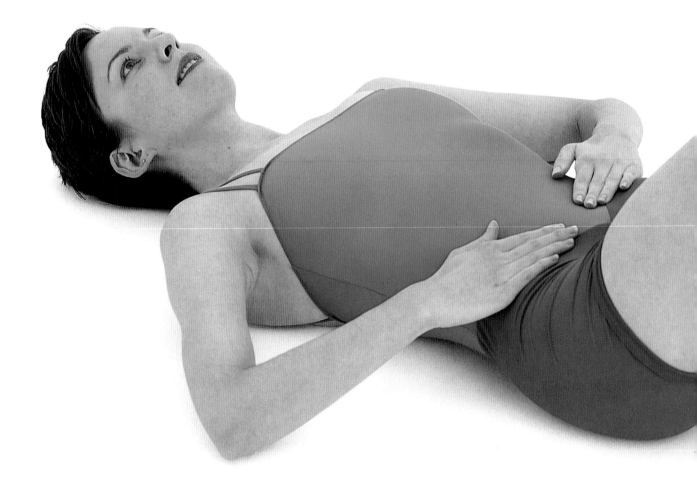

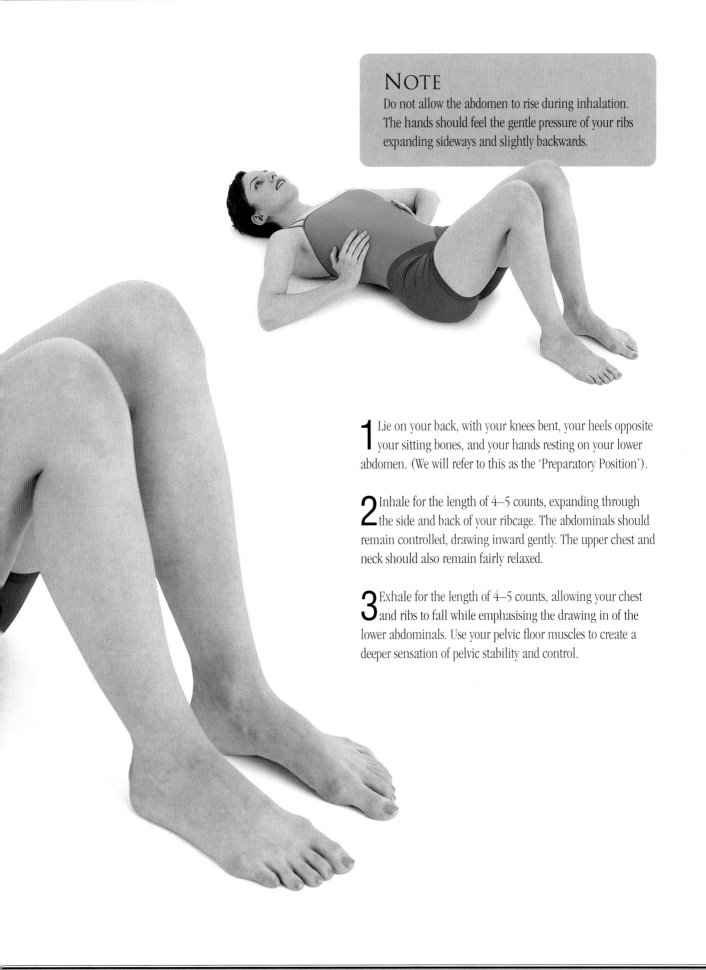

1 Lie on your back, with your knees bent, your heels opposite your sitting bones, and your hands resting on your lower abdomen. (We will refer to this as the 'Preparatory Position').

2 Inhale for the length of 4–5 counts, expanding through the side and back of your ribcage. The abdominals should remain controlled, drawing inward gently. The upper chest and neck should also remain fairly relaxed.

3 Exhale for the length of 4–5 counts, allowing your chest and ribs to fall while emphasising the drawing in of the lower abdominals. Use your pelvic floor muscles to create a deeper sensation of pelvic stability and control.

# POSTURE AWARENESS & PELVIC STABILITY

***Purpose*** *To challenge the ability to maintain a Neutral Pelvis Position and to develop abdominal and shoulder stability for postural endurance.*

# LEG SLIDES

**1** Begin in the Preparatory Position, inhale in order to prepare, and then begin 'scooping' the abdominals (as was described in Centring and Breathing).

**2** Exhale, sliding one heel along the floor, using your abdominals and maintaining control of your Neutral Pelvis Position.

**3** Inhale, dragging the heel back to the Preparatory Position, always maintaining abdominal bracing and pelvic stability.

**4** Repeat 10 times in all, alternating legs.

# POSTURE AWARENESS
# & PELVIC STABILITY

*(continued)*

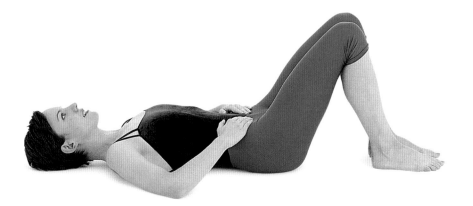

## LEG LIFTS

**1** Begin in the Preparatory Position, and then begin scooping the abdominals.

**2** Inhale as you lift your thigh towards the body so that your shin is parallel to the floor. Ensure deep abdominals and pelvic stability are your focus.

**3** Exhale, lowering your foot back to the floor, maintaining control of your abdominals and Neutral Pelvis.

**4** Repeat 10 times in all, alternating legs.

## PROGRESSION
Inhale, as you lift one leg. Exhale, lift the other.
Inhale, lower one down. Exhale, lower the other down.
Ensure abdominals do not pop up, or that your lower
back or pelvis release, as you lift the second leg.

# POSTURE AWARENESS
# & PELVIC STABILITY

*(continued)*

# SHOULDER STABILITY

**1** Begin in the Preparatory Position. Reach your arms towards the ceiling, with your shoulders drawing down.

**2** Inhale to reach your arms over your head, maintaining your natural spinal position. Be careful not to allow your ribs to lose contact with the floor, or your shoulders to shrug upward.

**3** Exhale, bringing your arms back towards the ceiling, emphasising your shoulders drawing down against the floor, and bracing your abdominals.

**4** Repeat 4–6 times, for general awareness of shoulder stability and coordination of abdominal and breath control.

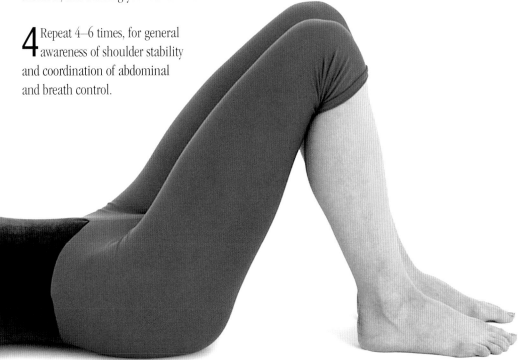

## PROGRESSION

To challenge your coordination, combine the Leg Slides and Shoulder Stability exercises. Inhale to slide your heel down as your arms reach overhead. Exhale to pull your leg and arms back to the Preparatory Position. Focus on abdominals and drawing your shoulders down, with no movement of the spine or pelvis.

# SPINAL MOBILITY

**_Purpose_** _Abdominal preparation, developing fluid spinal motion, and strengthening back, gluteals and hips._

# Pelvic Tilt

**1** Begin in the Preparatory Position, with your arms relaxed. Inhale laterally and begin scooping your abdominals.

**2** Exhale, drawing your lower abdominals inward to initiate a pelvic tilt backward, stretching your lower back. Make sure that your buttocks are relaxed and your feet are firmly planted on the floor.

**3** Inhale to roll your pelvis back to Neutral, and relax your hips completely.

**4** Repeat 4–5 times.

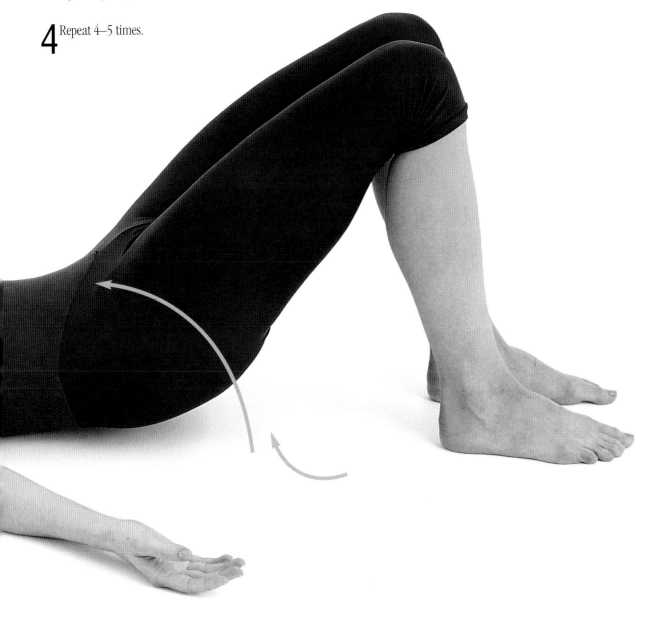

# Spinal Mobility

*(continued)*

## Pelvic Curl

**1** Begin as for the Pelvic Tilt.

**2** Exhale, scooping your lower abdominals to initiate a pelvic tilt backward, and roll your spine off the floor, aiming to articulate each segment. Use the muscles beneath your buttocks to lift your pelvis to eliminate any possibility of back strain.

**3** Inhale laterally, maintaining this position. Keep your feet firmly on the floor, your thighs parallel and neck and shoulders relaxed.

**4** Exhale, rolling the spine down to the floor with control. Maintain leg alignment and imagine lengthening the spine as it rolls.

**5** Inhale as you relax your hips completely.

**6** Repeat 5–6 times.

# Spinal Mobility

*(continued)*

## Knees Side-to-Side

**1** Part your feet until they are slightly wider than your pelvis, and prepare your abdominals.

**2** Inhale as you allow your thighs to gently fall to one side, causing the pelvis to roll sideways. Keep your shoulder blades on the floor.

**3** Emphasise your abdominals, exhaling as you roll the pelvis back to Neutral, with the legs following.

**4** Repeat 6–10 times in all, alternating sides.

# ABDOMINAL WARM-UP

**Purpose**  *Gentle abdominal work and developing breath control, while focusing on pelvic stability and leg alignment. These exercises are a preparation for subsequent exercises.*

## CHEST LIFT

**1** Begin in the Preparatory Position, with your hands behind your neck.

**2** Prepare by inhaling and scooping your abdominals.

**3** Exhale, lifting your head, neck and shoulders off the floor, pressing the abdominals towards your spine. Maintain Neutral Pelvis and resist overusing back, leg and gluteal muscles.

**4** Inhale laterally, maintaining abdominal flattening and chest height.

**5** Exhale, lowering your head and shoulders, and maintaining your abdominal scooping.

**6** Repeat 5–6 times.

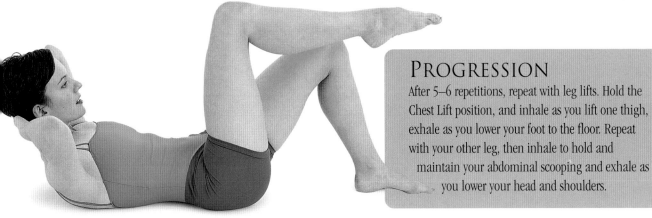

## PROGRESSION

After 5–6 repetitions, repeat with leg lifts. Hold the Chest Lift position, and inhale as you lift one thigh, exhale as you lower your foot to the floor. Repeat with your other leg, then inhale to hold and maintain your abdominal scooping and exhale as you lower your head and shoulders.

# ABDOMINAL WARM-UP

*(continued)*

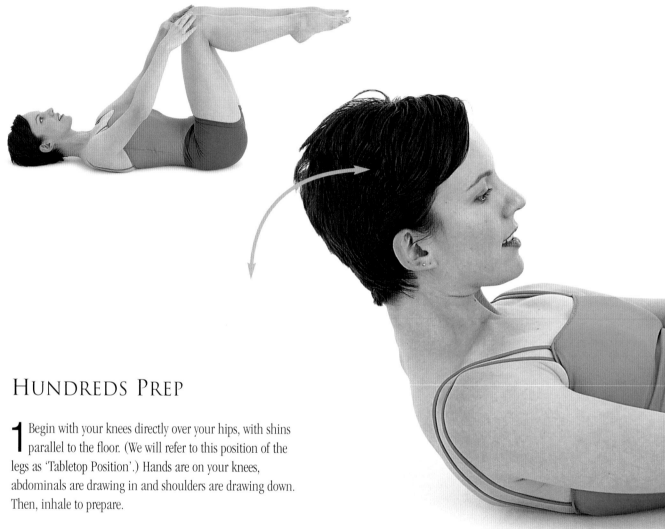

## HUNDREDS PREP

**1** Begin with your knees directly over your hips, with shins parallel to the floor. (We will refer to this position of the legs as 'Tabletop Position'.) Hands are on your knees, abdominals are drawing in and shoulders are drawing down. Then, inhale to prepare.

**2** Exhale to emphasise abdominal scooping as the head and shoulders lift, reaching the arms down past your hips. Do not lose control of the Neutral Pelvis Position, or allow your stomach to pop up.

**3** Inhale laterally, as you lower your head and shoulders while maintaining abdominal control. Bring your hands back to your knees.

**4** Repeat 5–6 times.

If your abdominals are weak, or you experience back pain, rest your feet on a chair while curling up and down. Alternatively, your physician may recommend that you do not execute any exercises where both legs are in the air.

## PROGRESSION

Once you are achieving a curl and maintaining absolute pelvic stability and flat abdominals, try extending your legs upward as you curl and reach both arms down by your sides. Bend your knees fractionally before lowering the head and shoulders to protect your back from arching off the floor.

# ABDOMINAL WARM-UP

*(continued)*

## HUNDREDS

**1** Begin as we did for the Breathing Exercise. There are a few progressions from the basic breathing to challenge your abdominal and breath control.

**2** If you can maintain correct abdominal flattening and have no back pain, raise your legs to the Tabletop Position and repeat the breathing (4–5 counts in, 4–5 counts out). If this is too difficult, rest your heels on a chair to help support the weight of your legs.

**3** *Next progression*—maintaining the legs at Tabletop, lift your head and shoulders and reach both arms down by your hips. Continue the same breathing pattern and use small arm movements (pulsing up and down) to maintain a rhythm for your breath and counting. Build up to 10 full breaths in this manner, as you develop greater abdominal stamina and control.

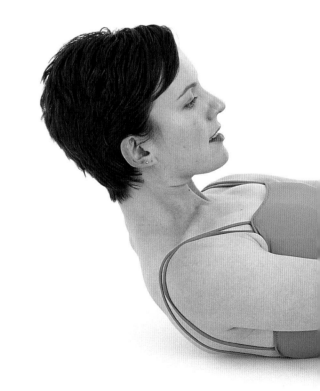

## PROGRESSION

Step 3 is a classic Pilates exercise known as Hundreds. As you gain strength, extend your legs toward the ceiling and slightly away from you. Remember to keep scooping your abdominals and maintain a stable Neutral Pelvis Position. Don't progress yourself to the extended leg position until you are ready.

# ABDOMINAL WARM-UP

*(continued)*

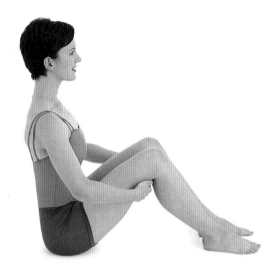

## ROLL UP PREP

**1** Start in a seated position, with your legs bent in front of you and slightly apart. Hold your hands gently beneath your knees. Sit up straight with your shoulders down and abdominals scooping in and upward, and then inhale to prepare.

**2** Exhale, pulling your navel toward your spine to initiate a pelvic tilt backward so that you can roll back sufficiently to challenge the abdominals—without losing the round lower back position. Ensure that the abdominals are working, and not the legs or arms!

**3** Inhale laterally, to hold still, deepening the abdominals without other physical tensions.

**4** Exhale to roll forward to resume the seated position. Again, ensure that it is actually the abdominals that move you.

**5** Repeat 6–10 times, being careful to roll only to a position in which you can maintain full abdominal control.

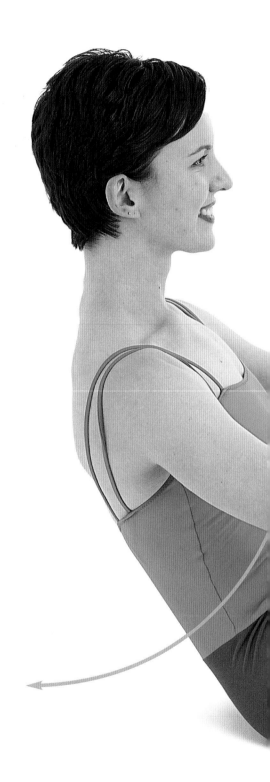

## PROGRESSION
Take your hands away and simply reach forward at shoulder height. Be careful not to allow the shoulders to rise, or to lean back without rolling first.

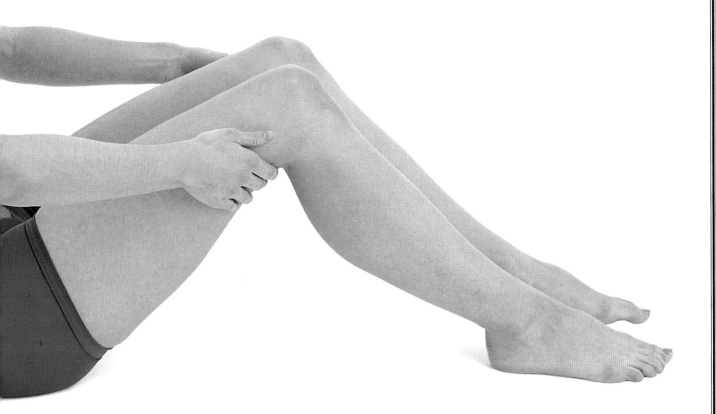

# ABDOMINAL
# STRENGTHENING

**Purpose**  *To further challenge the abdominals
and the stability of the pelvis while limbs or
upper torso are moving.*

# OBLIQUE LIFTS

**1** Begin in the Preparatory Position, with your hands behind your head and neck. Then, inhale to prepare.

**2** Exhale as the head and shoulders lift, rotating your upper torso and pressing the abdominals down to establish a strong position of the pelvis and waistline. Your pelvis and legs should not move.

**3** Inhale as you lower back to the floor. Maintain your abdominal scooping action and imagine lengthening your spine.

**4** Repeat 8–10 times, alternating sides.

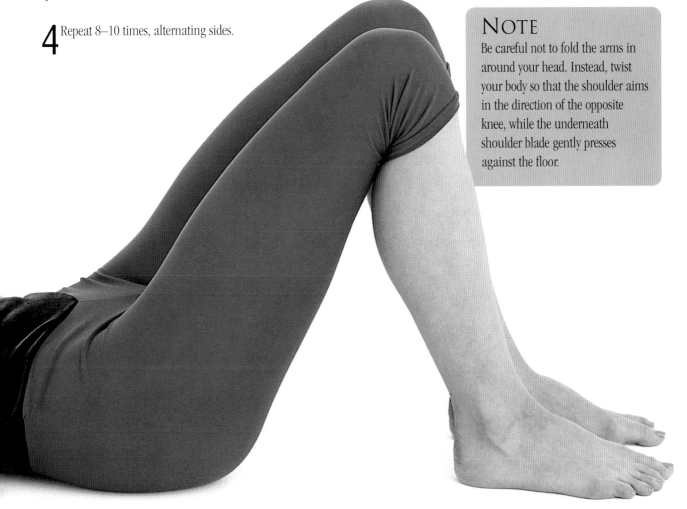

## NOTE
Be careful not to fold the arms in around your head. Instead, twist your body so that the shoulder aims in the direction of the opposite knee, while the underneath shoulder blade gently presses against the floor.

# ABDOMINAL STRENGTHENING

*(continued)*

## SINGLE LEG STRETCH

**1** Lie on your back, with your legs in the Tabletop Position and hands on your knees. Inhale to prepare and start scooping the abdominals.

**2** Exhale as one leg extends upward and away from your body, maintaining abdominals and drawing your shoulders down.

**3** Inhale as you draw the leg back. Try to emphasise scooping your abdominals on each inhalation, as this is the preparation for the next leg extension!

**4** Exhale as you extend the other leg.

**5** Repeat 8–10 times, alternating legs.

## PROGRESSION
For additional abdominal work, curl your head and shoulders off the floor throughout.

# SPINAL ROTATION

***Purpose*** *To encourage correct muscular support as the spine executes a rotatory movement, while managing pelvic and shoulder girdle stability.*

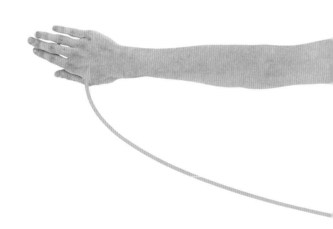

## SPINE TWIST

**1** Sit tall, with both legs either extended straight out in front of your body, or crossed. (This depends on deciding which is the best position for you to sit in without slumping in the lower back. A small box or chair may be needed to relieve pressure on your lower back, enabling this upright posture.)

**2** Extend your arms sideways at shoulder height, palms turned backward and shoulders drawing down. Anchor your hips to the floor, and if the legs are straight in front, bring your knees and ankles firmly together. This will help maintain your sense of pelvic stability.

**3** Inhale to 'grow' tall, abdominals drawing in and upward, shoulders down.

**4** Exhale as you twist from the waist with a double pulse action. Ensure that your hips don't rotate or lift, and that your shoulders don't rise or drop on one side! Imagine spiralling the spine upwards.

**5** Inhale as you return to the centre, maintaining a tall seated position. Remember to breathe laterally and to keep drawing your abdominals in and upward.

**6** Repeat 8–10 times, alternating sides.

# SIDE STABILITY, GLUTEALS & INSIDE THIGHS

**Purpose**  *Strengthening of the side, hip and inside thigh muscles, while still maintaining abdominal and postural support. Since it's more difficult to balance when lying on the side, this is also a position which is useful to challenge and develop spinal and pelvic stability.*

# SIDE LEG LIFTS

**1** Lie on one side with both legs extending longways and slightly forward of your body. When on the side, one hip bone should be directly vertically aligned with the other. Place the hand of your top arm on the floor in front of your torso—this is a gentle reminder to use the abdominals to stabilise you, and is not there to prop you up!

**2** Inhale to prepare and stabilise your torso with the abdominals.

**3** Exhale, lengthening both legs away and lifting them just clear of the floor.

**4** Inhale as you lower them.

**5** Repeat 10 times, each side, ensuring that your lower back doesn't arch or strain.

## NOTE
If this is too difficult, or if back pain is experienced, start by lifting only your top leg a few inches and maintaining focus on your abdominals for side balancing.

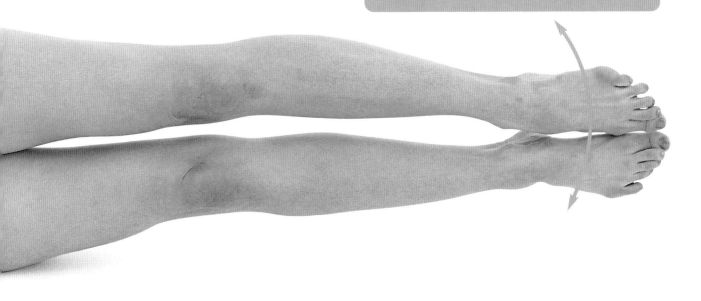

# SIDE STABILITY, GLUTEALS & INSIDE THIGHS

*(continued)*

# WALL GLUTES

**1** Lie on one side, as if your torso were against a wall. Maintain all the crucial curves of the spine and place your underneath leg forward of your body, bent, for stability. Your top leg is extended longways, though not rigid. Your thigh should relax inward slightly.

**2** Exhale as you lift your leg slightly and hold momentarily. Maintain absolute pelvic stability, lifting predominately from the back of your hip.

**3** Inhale as you slowly lower your leg.

**4** Repeat 10–15 times each side.

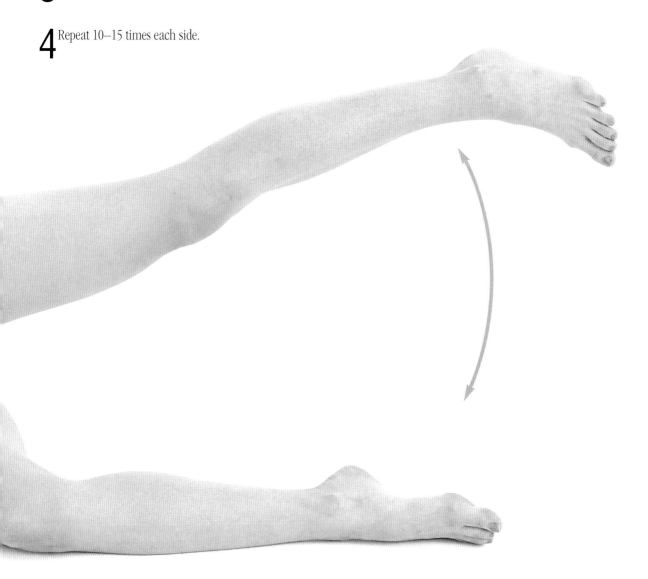

# SIDE STABILITY, GLUTEALS & INSIDE THIGHS

*(continued)*

## CUSHION SQUEEZE

**1** Begin in the Preparatory Position, with a cushion placed between your thighs. Inhale to prepare the abdominals.

**2** Exhale as you emphasise your abdominals drawing in and upward and squeeze your thighs together. Focus on abdominals and inside thighs—keep your gluteal muscles fairly relaxed, and ensure a Neutral Pelvis Position is maintained.

**3** Inhale as you hold the squeeze, maintaining abdominals.

**4** Exhale as you release the cushion.

**5** Repeat 8–10 times.

# SCAPULA STABILITY & BACK STRENGTHENING

**Purpose** *Correct scapula (shoulder blade) and shoulder positioning is necessary to develop endurance of the postural muscles. When the middle and upper back become stronger, stress is reduced for the neck and shoulder joints.*

# ARM RAISES (FRONT & SIDE)

**1** Begin sitting or standing. Lengthen your spine, draw abdominals in and upward and gently pull your shoulders back to broaden the chest. Start with your arms relaxed by your sides, with the palms of your hands facing the body.

**2** Inhale, raising your arms forward while maintaining the shoulder blades in a flat position. Only raise your arms to a height where the shoulder blades don't protrude, or 'wing', and the shoulders don't shrug upward.

**3** Exhale as you lower your arms.

**4** Repeat 8–10 times.

# SCAPULA STABILITY & BACK STRENGTHENING

*(continued)*

## ARM RAISES (CONTINUED)

**5** Repeat with your arms lifting sideways, though slightly forward of your torso. Palms of the hands should now be facing the front, and your shoulder blades should still remain flat. Ensuring that the abdominals still draw in and upward, keep a sense of length through the waist, and calmness in the neck and upper chest. Imagine a trickle of water running down the centre of your upper back. A feeling of strength and bracing should be felt there.

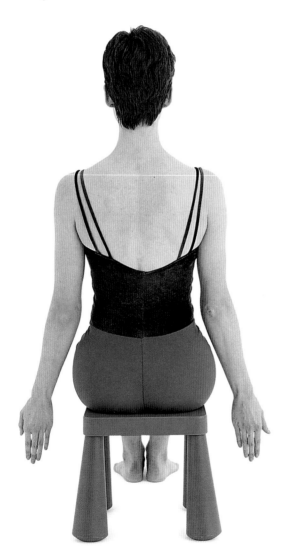

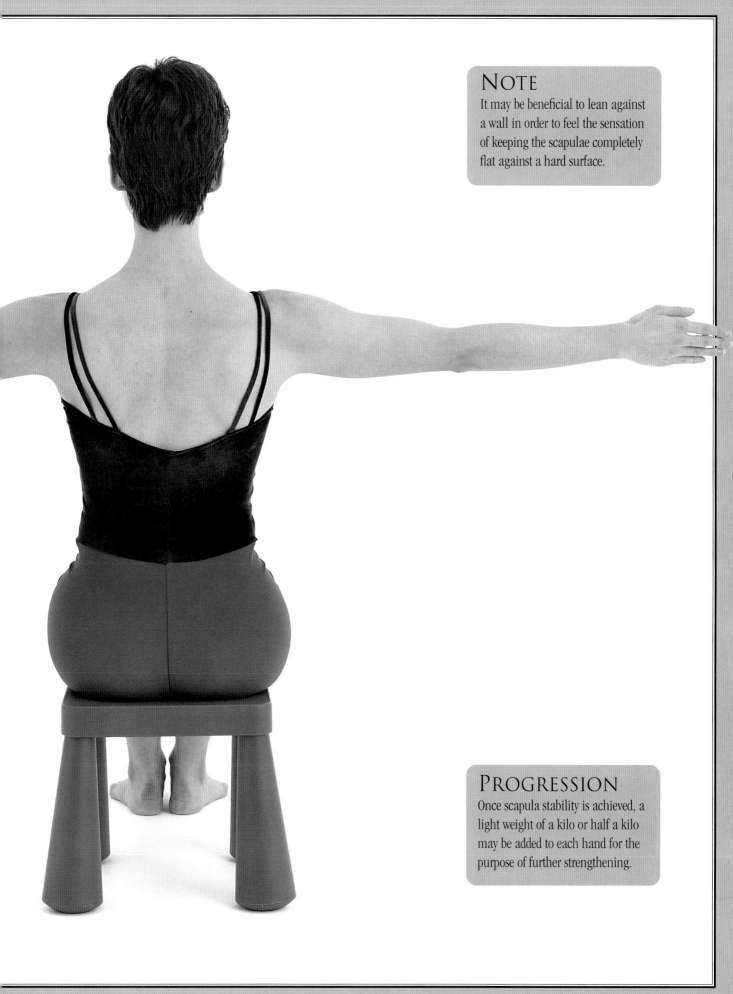

# SCAPULA STABILITY & BACK STRENGTHENING

*(continued)*

## BACK EXTENSION

**1** Lie face down, arms beside your body and forehead resting on a small cushion, or rolled towel. Without altering your natural back position, draw your lower abdominals deep up toward the spine. Inhale to prepare.

**2** Exhale, drawing the shoulders and hands back as if pressing against a wall when standing. Maintain your abdominals and upper back 'bracing' while keeping the chest and ribs on the floor (head and shoulders 'hover' off the floor).

**3** Inhale, holding this position. Keep your nose pointing toward the floor so that your neck remains in line with the rest of the spine. Maintain abdominals. Reach toward the toes.

**4** Exhale as you rest.

**5** Repeat 8–10 times.

## NOTE
Ensure that the abdominal muscles are stabilising strongly—not the gluteals or legs!

# FULL BODY INTEGRATION

***Purpose*** *Here are a couple of preparations for some full-body challenges, the Pilates way. Relying on the deep abdominals, back and hip muscles, these two exercises are primers for movement that requires abdominal strength, flexibility and muscle control.*

## TEASER PREP BALANCE

**1** Begin in a sitting position, with your knees bent, your hands under the thighs and feet lightly placed on the floor.

**2** Roll back onto your tailbone and stabilise the position with your abdominals. Your feet should hover just off the floor, as you maintain abdominals and try to limit muscle tension in the thighs. Shoulders are relaxed.

**3** Focus on breathing naturally and laterally. Keep scooping your abdominals and maintain a constant distance between the chest and knees.

**4** Maintain this position, while breathing, for 6–8 breaths.

**5** On the next inhalation, raise your shins so they become parallel with the floor—not allowing your torso or thigh position to change. More abdominals!

**6** Exhale as you control the lowering of your shins.

**7** Repeat 6–8 times.

# FULL BODY INTEGRATION

*(continued)*

## ROLL OVERS

**1** Lie on your back, with your legs together and stretched toward the ceiling, and your arms by your sides. Inhale to prepare the abdominals. Depending on your hamstring flexibility, you may need to bend your knees a little.

**2** Exhale as you use the abdominals strongly to lift your legs and hips up and over your head. Ensure that you don't strain with your neck, shoulders and arms. Abdominals should not pop out.

**3** Inhale as you flex your feet and separate them to shoulder width while your legs remain parallel to the floor.

**4** Exhale, rolling through your spine one vertebra at a time, abdominals controlling the movement. Your neck and shoulders should be as relaxed as possible.

**5** Finish the roll, returning the pelvis back to Neutral and then inhale as the legs come back together, stretch them to the ceiling, and prepare to repeat.

**6** Repeat 5–6 times.

## NOTE
This exercise is unsuitable for people with neck or lower back injuries.

# STRETCHES

*Purpose* During and following muscle work, stretching helps muscles recover. There is also a definite need to develop a balance of strength with flexibility in order to reduce the risk of injury or strain. Lengthened muscles have the capacity to gain more strength and create a lithe, streamlined physique.

## NOTE

All stretches are to be held for 3–4 breaths to allow the muscles time to relax. Repeat for the other side, then repeat both sides again. If unnecessary strain is present, reduce or stop the stretch and consult your physician.

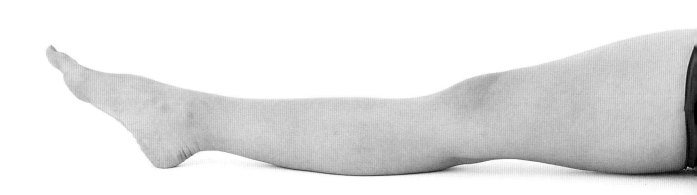

## HAMSTRINGS

Lie on your back holding a towel around one foot, and the other leg stretched along the floor. Maintain a Neutral Pelvis Position and gently pull the raised leg toward you, aiming your heel toward the ceiling.

# STRETCHES

*(continued)*

## QUADRICEPS

L ie on your side, with your underneath knee bent and
pulled up toward your chest. Hold the foot of the top leg
behind you, with your thigh parallel to the floor. Pull your
foot to achieve a stretch at the front of your thigh. Gently push
the top hip forward as you pull your thigh back. Brace with
the abdominals.

## GLUTEALS (BUTTOCKS)

Lying on your back, cross one ankle over the other knee and pull both legs toward you, ensuring that your tailbone does not leave the floor. Keep your hips as square as possible, and relax the hip muscles.

# STRETCHES

*(continued)*

## HIP FLEXORS

Kneel on one knee with the other leg bent and in front of your body. Both legs should remain aligned with the hips, with both hip bones facing front. Draw your abdominals in and upward, tilting the pelvis backward (as you did in the Pelvic Curl exercise) and lean slightly forward—resist sinking into your lower back, but keep 'zipping up' the abdominals and the front of the stretching hip.

# Neck

Sit, comfortably, with upright posture. Allow your head to tilt directly to one side—'ear to shoulder'. The opposite shoulder gently pulls downward.

# GLOSSARY FOR MUSCLE TERMINOLOGY

## GLUTEALS
Muscle group of the buttocks, that contribute to hip movement and pelvic/back stability.

## HAMSTRINGS
Muscle group of the back of the thigh, from the hip to the knee, that bend the knee or assist in backward leg motion.

## HIP FLEXORS
Muscles at the front of the hip that lift the thigh towards the torso.

## OBLIQUE ABDOMINALS
The side muscles of the abdomen that twist, or rotate, the torso.

## QUADRICEPS
Muscle group of the front of the thigh, from the hip to the knee, that makes up the major muscle mass of the thigh.

# CONCLUSION

The Pilates Method has emerged from various philosophies that endorse physical health and longevity. This technique of conditioning the body and mind was developed with the intention to re-create an individual's approach to exercise and fitness in general. Far beyond the 'no pain, no gain' mentality of working the body, Pilates enforces muscle control and endurance without resulting in post-exercise soreness and fatigue. This method is suitable for all ages and levels of fitness. It incorporates all the essential concepts in order to achieve postural and lifestyle improvements and sports-specific cross-training benefits and provides a way in which to learn about your body and develop greater levels of agility, energy and concentration.

# MORE
## SIMPLY
# PILATES

Assistant Coordinator: Rodney Searle
Art Director: Karen Moores
Graphic Artist: Susie Allen
Photographer: Glenn Weiss

# CONTENTS

# INTRODUCTION

Pilates is often described as the 'intelligent workout' as it is a movement-based discipline that also aligns itself with the 'less is more' exercise principle.

Although the Pilates Method was developed almost a century ago, recognition of its many benefits has grown during recent years. In the early 1900s, German-born Joseph Pilates devised a system of movement, undertaken in a particular sequence, that would achieve and maintain an individual's optimal level of overall mind/body fitness. The basis of his philosophy came from his knowledge of various exercise principles. Following his death in the 1960s, Joseph's legacy was continued initially by his students, and has evolved over the years into various and similar forms, though the principles remain the same.

People from all walks of life have gained benefit from the Method. Dancers and celebrities have long been known to incorporate Pilates into their lifestyle schedule. This continuing trend amongst the rich, famous and beautiful has led to recent mainstream popularity of the Method.

While a strong, toned and elongated body is frequently the sought after reward for many fitness conscious individuals, any aesthetic value in muscle development is actually a secondary bonus to the functional musculo-skeletal benefits gained from a sensible and committed approach to the Pilates Method.

When practised as it was intended – as a postural retraining method, both generally and through movement – Pilates exercises help restore symmetry to the body, thus aiding in the development of, or restoring of, balanced strength up to any level attainable.

The Pilates Method is a system of movement-based mind-body conditioning exercises. It is suitable for everyone from people with general and rehabilitative needs through to the elite athlete, providing the individual applies their concentration and imagination! As strengthening the muscles supports the joints, a growing number of physical practitioners regard the Pilates Method as an appropriate complement to the treatment and prevention of injury.

'Less is more' with sensible exercising, so restrict the number of repetitions of each exercise – in accordance with your ability – to maintain correct form. If you experience joint pain, seek advice from a qualified professional rather than pushing through the pain barrier!

# BENEFITS

A regular 'mind-body conditioning routine' should be considered a wise investment in the future of our health. As we age, our bodies succumb to natural degenerative changes. However, choosing to incorporate a 'holistic approach' to exercising will maintain your optimal mobility and agility.

Pilates mat work re-educates an individual how to best place, move and coordinate their body. Like any worthwhile endeavour, this is obviously a process that's difficult to improve upon, if there is no real commitment to practice! Pilates is a 'way' of exercising as much as it is a sequence of exercises...and the benefits are many and effective, regardless of age or fitness level.

Pilates is all about restoring balance and symmetry throughout the body – ie, the stability and mobility of joints; and the suppleness and strength of muscles.

Furthermore, regular practise of the Pilates philosophy will promote relaxation, complete body control, movement articulation and coordination, as well as increased energy levels and a more confident posture.

The versatility of Pilates exercises for different fitness needs is also widely recognised. Greater confidence and coordination in movement execution for both functional (general, everyday movement) and specific/sophisticated means (such as sports) is certainly achievable.

*More Simply Pilates* will draw your attention to the benefits of moving the body in a methodical and articulate manner, allowing you to gain abdominal, back and hip strength in a way that is safe for your spine. You will experience greater control over movement and breathing, and your strength gained will give a true sense of stability with elongated muscle tone, rather than superficial muscle bulk. In addition, your posture will become more effortless from the strength and mobility exercises for your upper back and shoulders.

# PILATES PRINCIPLES

The following fundamental points are based on Joseph Pilates' beliefs outlining how the movement is to be executed, in order to achieve the benefits it does. Pilates is 'pilates' because of the 'way' the exercises are articulately done. Integrating these principles into the way you move is exercising 'intelligently' for the longevity of your body.

- Concentration • Control • Centring
- Fluidity • Precision • Breathing

Because Pilates is very much a mind workout – requiring inward focus and concentration on a number of things at once – the movement is often taught by the use of 'images'. A vivid imagination is an advantage when learning the Pilates 'way' of body conditioning. Imagery is a powerful tool in assisting an individual to correctly execute and articulate the exercises. This helps facilitate a deeper, more kinesthetic awareness of musculoskeletal mechanics and movement dynamics. Visualisation also assists with breathing flow and/or dynamics. It is important to realise how Pilates is not about 'working hard' and 'burning' your muscles. That may come after you achieve the fundamentals! You want to train your mind first – body awareness is a must so that your journey with the Pilates Method can be one of 'discovering' how you can get your body to move with the greatest of ease.

# PRACTICAL MATTERS

There are generally a set of standard Pilates mat exercises which are traditionally broken up into 'basic', 'intermediate' and 'advanced' levels of difficulty. It is important to realise your own physical capabilities when embarking on any new activity. Concentrate on the quality of your personal execution of an exercise sequence and not on the choreography of fancy movement. Pilates is a 'sensible approach' to correcting and maintaining postural alignment, strength and suppleness. Try to regard your practise of Pilates much like 'building blocks' – master your abilities step by step and don't execute movement sequences that may cause you to forego correct placement and stability.

Firstly read and acknowledge the information relating to correct abdominal bracing and body alignment and then proceed with the workout at a pace suitable to your fitness level.

In the case of injury, or physical limitations, seek advice from your physical practitioner prior to starting any new exercise program. Pilates is not recommended if you are pregnant unless you have previously been attending regular sessions and you have clearance from your doctor. Your qualified Pilates instructor may develop an appropriate workout program for you. Depending on what your physical life entails, two to four Pilates workouts a week is optimal, as it's the consistency that will ensure full benefit. Remember, the 'less is more' philosophy with sensible exercising.

## Requirements

You will need certain accessories in order to do your Pilates mat workout. The mat or carpet surface must offer some comfort, but must not be so soft that your body sinks into it, as this causes your spine to lose the integrity of its natural curvature. In addition, you will need a small pillow and a towel to assist you with some exercises and stretches. (You may also use these to rest your head and neck upon for support.) Finally, it is recommended that you use a low chair or box to relieve lower back tension during some of the 'sitting' exercises.

# CENTRING AND BREATHING

*Always commence your Pilates workout quietly, focusing on some important concepts that will be your priority during the exercises so that you can maximise the benefits.*

NEUTRAL PELVIS is a term that describes the position of the pelvis when the spine is in its natural position. Usually, your hip bones (iliac crests) and your pubic bone should form a parallel level with the floor. Your lower back should not be pressed into the floor, nor should it be over arched. This creates the best position for your deeper abdominal muscles to be strengthened.

BREATHING is important to focus on, but don't become consumed by the need to breathe too deeply or artificially just to do the exercises. Breathe normally, accenting the exhale, and try to develop a different way of breathing that will help you keep 'control' of your abdominal muscles. In Pilates we call this 'lateral breathing', which means to direct the breath into the side and back of the lower ribcage.

ABDOMINAL ACTIVATION in Pilates is a major priority. It is not about the sheer effort of contracting these muscles, but rather the subtleness of refining how you do so. Don't ever clench your muscles or allow the stomach to pop up. Draw the muscles of the pelvic floor up and gently press the lower abdominals to the spine.

Your deep abdominal muscles act like reinforcement for the joints of your spine. When you combine this action with regular breathing, make sure your neck is relaxed and your ribs don't protrude. Imagine a pin at the base of your ribs while you breathe laterally and simply scoop your lower abdominals inward and upward. With each exhale, imagine your waist shrinking.

# CENTRING AND BREATHING

*(continued)*

PREPARATORY NOTE: The essence of Pilates starts with the placement of your pelvis, ribcage, scapulae (shoulder blades) and head – as movement or displacement of any, or all of these effects the curves of the spine. Once you are 'aligned' then turn your focus to the coordination of your breath and abdominal bracing action. The Method is all about maintaining a posture that is simple and natural; maintaining a natural breathing rhythm and learning how to facilitate gentle and effective abdominal bracing for lumbo-pelvic stability.

Movement on any level comes after this awareness of 'stabilising' the torso. Your limbs should be easily mobile without losing a strong sense of 'centre' – referred to now as 'core stability'. Joseph Pilates referred to the muscles around the 'centre' as the 'powerhouse'.

## BREATHING EXERCISE

**1** Lie on your back with your legs bent and heels in line with your sitting bones. (This position will be referred to as a 'preparatory' position, as all exercises that begin on your back must start in a neutral alignment.)

**2** Rest your hands on your abdomen and draw your attention to how you are breathing. As you inhale visualise doing so through the back and sides of your lower ribcage so that your deep abdominal muscles can remain braced. Try not to elevate your shoulders or change the shape of your spine.

**3** As you exhale, emphasise a deeper drawing in action of your lower abdominals. Try to imagine the front of your spine, especially where it joins the pelvis. Lift your pelvic floor muscles and scoop your deep lower abdominal muscles (like an 'inward-upward' action) in order to give you a sensation of stabilising the lower back.

# WARM UP

**Purpose**  *The warm up enables you to establish and practise the basic principles of Pilates with simple movements. This is also preparing you for subsequent exercises.*

## HIP MOBILITY

**1** Start in your preparatory position. As you breathe in, open one knee to the side and slide the same foot directly away from your sitting bone. Straighten this leg and aim to keep both hips still on the floor and keep your other leg tension free. Do not arch your back.

**2** Exhale, rotating your leg inward and drawing the heel back toward your sitting bone. Keep your ribcage fairly flat on the floor, your pelvis anchored and your abdominals flat and strong.

**3** Repeat on the same side in the same direction. Do 3-4 repetitions of these in each direction, with each leg.

# Warm Up

*(continued)*

## Leg Floats

**1** Start in your preparatory position with your abdominal muscles braced. Inhale as you lift one knee toward you, keeping the shin bone parallel to the floor.

**2** Exhale as you extend the leg away from you, only as far as you can keep your pelvis and ribcage still and symmetrical. Visualise shrinking through your waist and pulling your navel area to your spine.

**3** Breathe in as you bend your leg back toward you, maintaining the lift of your pelvic floor and deep abdominals.

**4** Exhale as you replace the foot to the floor.

**5** Alternate legs for 6-10 repetitions.

### Note
Remember not to focus too much on limb movement. The movement develops your coordination and challenges your trunk stability, while you gain abdominal strength and endurance in preparation for later exercises.

# WARM UP

*(continued)*

## SCAPULA MOVEMENT

1 Stay in your preparatory position and raise your arms toward the ceiling, slightly wider than shoulder width apart. Nod your chin gently and maintain a sense of stability around your waist.

2 As you inhale, reach your arms toward the ceiling to produce movement of the shoulder blades 'forward', while not affecting your neck position. Your shoulders should not elevate toward your head.

3 Breathe out (keep reaching your fingers up to create some resistance) as you retract your shoulders down toward the back of your waist, without moving your ribcage or head and neck.

4 Continue for 6-10 repetitions.

NOTE
This exercise will assist you in learning how to best stabilise your shoulder blades as they are required to sit flat against the back of your ribcage throughout many of the Pilates exercises. This strengthens your middle back muscles for better posture.

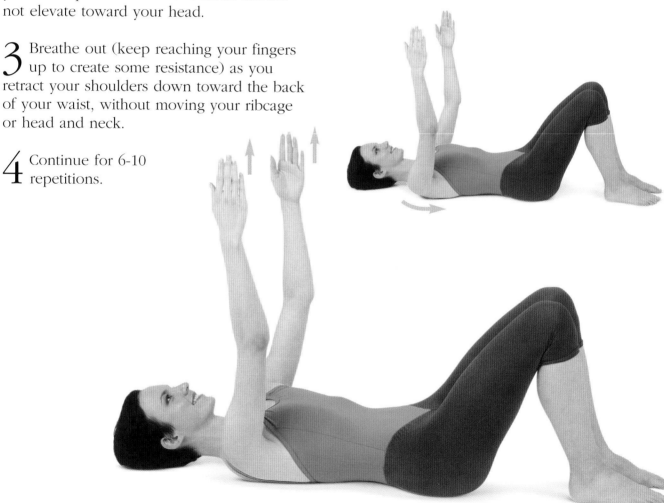

## ARM CIRCLES

1 Begin as you did for Scapula Movement. Inhale as you take your arms overhead without moving your ribcage or shoulder blades.

2 As you exhale, face your palms toward the ceiling and draw your arms, in a wide circle, down to your sides. Keep your chest open so you don't become round shouldered and remember to maintain taut abdominals.

3 Repeat 3-5 times, then reverse the circles.

# WARM UP

*(continued)*

## CHEST LIFT

**1** Stay in your preparatory alignment and place your hands behind your head, keeping both elbows within your vision. Draw your shoulder blades down, keeping your ribcage and pelvis anchored to the floor and shrink through your abdominal area. Inhale.

**2** As you exhale, roll your chest forward, dropping your chin gently and pressing your lower ribcage down toward the floor. Keep your legs relaxed and your pelvis anchored on the floor.

**3** Inhale, hold still and strong, being careful not to allow your ribs to release from the floor or your abdomen to 'pop' up. Visualise breathing into your back and keep your shoulders stable.

**4** Roll down as you exhale, keep scooping your abdominals toward your spine so that you develop variations in strength.

**5** Repeat 5-10 times.

> **NOTE**
> The Chest Lift is the basis of more advanced Pilates abdominal work and your priority is to address all the fundamental principles outlined so far.

# Double Leg Slides

**1** Maintain the preparatory position. Place your hands on your hip and waist region so that you will be aware if any unnecessary movement occurs. Breathe in, drawing your deep abdominals inward and upward like an internal zip.

**2** As you exhale, slide both feet directly away from you, emphasising a slight pressing down of the abdomen and lower back toward the floor, so that you reinforce your spine.

**3** Breathe in, maintaining your posture. Ensure that your shoulder blades are drawn down and your ribs stay on the floor.

**4** Slide your heels back toward your sitting bones as you exhale. Visualise a connection between your shoulders drawing down, abdominals shrinking and your lower ribcage pressing into the floor.

**5** Repeat 3-5 times before combining with the Chest Lift exercise.

# WARM UP

*(continued)*

## DOUBLE LEG SLIDES *(continued)*

**6** Start as you would for Chest Lift. Inhale.

**7** Exhale, roll forward, pressing your lower ribs toward the floor and shrink through your waist. Inhale, hold still.

**8** Exhale as you slide your feet away – only as far as you can maintain your Chest Lift position. Don't allow your back or pelvis to move. Inhale, hold.

**9** As you exhale draw your heels back toward you. Keep your shoulders drawing down and emphasise scooped in abdominals. Inhale, hold.

**10** Exhale as you roll back down.

**11** Repeat 3-5 times.

### NOTE
Remember that your Warm Up exercises should be treated as the blueprint for more difficult exercises. Keep your pelvis and ribcage stable and your waist and shoulders strong. Start to elongate your exhales to facilitate a deeper sense of abdominal strength.

# CHEST LIFT HOLDING

**1** Begin as for the Chest Lift. Breathe in, preparing your abdominal muscles, careful not to arch your ribs off the floor.

**2** As you exhale, roll your chest forward without moving your pelvis.

**3** Maintain this position and continue breathing calmly. With each inhale, don't allow yourself to lie down at all and with each exhale, emphasise deeper abdominals and shoulders down. Relax your thighs and hips.

**4** Continue breathing; count 5-6 inhales. Exhale, roll down.

# Warm Up

*(continued)*

## Hundred

**1** Begin in your preparatory position. Lift one leg at a time to a 'tabletop' position. Feel that the back of your pelvis and ribcage are anchored on the floor, that your shoulders are relaxed and that your abdominals are zipped firmly. Assume a calm breathing pattern. Place your arms by your sides.

**2** As you exhale, nod your chin down gently and roll your ribcage forward, reaching your arms alongside you just off the floor. Press your stomach deep toward your spine, stabilising your hip bones on the floor. Extend your legs only as far as your trunk is stable, or maintain the legs at tabletop.

**3** Keep this position strong and continue to breathe, though in a broken breath pattern. Inhale, two short breaths and exhale, two short breaths. Accent the second inhale and exhale of each breath. Inhale, *inhale,* exhale, *exhale…*

**4** Continue breathing for 10 full breaths. Maintain a pure and stable position, emphasising the need for firm, flat abdominals and depressing the shoulder blades. Before you lie down bend your knees toward your chest to protect the lower back.

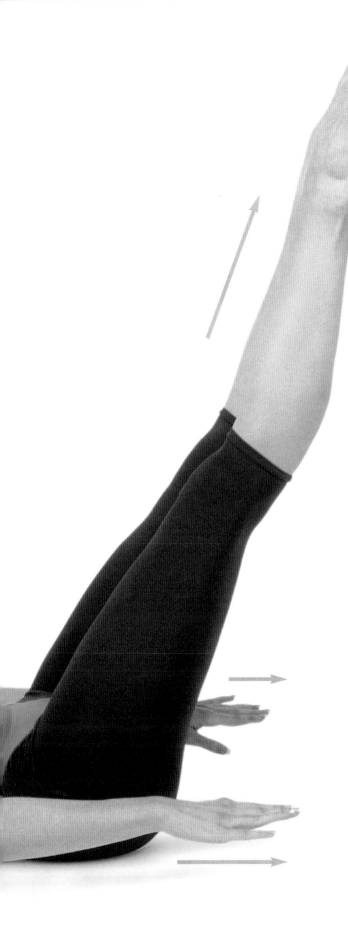

NOTE
Realise the transition from the initial
Breathing Exercise, to Chest Lift Holding
and now to the Hundred. Learn to
coordinate your diaphragm and deep
abdominal muscles so that you develop
a strong 'centre' and abdominal stamina.
Throughout this process always
endeavour to relax the muscles you
don't need to use.

MODIFICATION
If you have a vulnerable neck and back,
or if you lack strength, the Hundred is
still suitable to practise with your head
down (on a pillow if necessary) and
your feet resting on a chair. This is an
appropriate exercise as an extension
to the Breathing Exercise, as you can
develop core abdominal strength in a
gentle manner.

# WARM UP

*(continued)*

## ROLL UP (PREP & FULL)

1 Start sitting with your legs comfortably bent in front of you and your hands at the back of your thighs. Lengthen your spine, lift your abdominal muscles inward and upward... and drop your shoulders. Breathe in.

2 As you exhale, pull your deep abdominals further toward your spine so that your pelvis can easily roll away from your thighs. Relax your thigh muscles (and use your arms if necessary) as you train your abdominals to articulate spinal movement.

3 Inhale, maintaining the round shape of your spine and strong centre.

4 As you exhale, rock forward toward your legs, keeping the spine and pelvis in exactly the same position. This resembles the top part of a typical 'sit up', so train your abdominals to stabilise your spine.

5 Repeat 3-5 times. Use your arms to assist the movement if your abdominals are struggling.

6 For the full Roll Up, roll your pelvis back from your thighs as you exhale and continue rolling through the back of your waist, then your ribcage and finally allow your head to touch the floor. Reach your arms overhead to stretch the shoulders and challenge your spinal stability.

7 Inhale, raising your arms to the ceiling. Draw the shoulders down, ribs down and shrink the waist.

8 Drop your chin gently and as you exhale roll forward, pressing the ribs into the floor, then press your abdominals very deeply toward your spine as you continue to roll forward to a sitting position.

9 Inhale, emphasise the drawing back of your abdominals and begin to roll your hip bones away from your thighs. Keep your shoulders relaxed.

10 Repeat 3-5 times. Continue to use your arms if you need assistance with a smooth rolling action. Straighten your legs as you become stronger to challenge pelvic stability and fluid spinal movement. Be conscious not to miss out on rolling through the lumbar spine.

NOTE
Remember how important symmetry is throughout the body. Ensure that you roll evenly through the spine – with left and right sides equal – and no jerky movements.

# ABDOMINAL STRENGTHENING

***Purpose*** *The essence of Pilates is strengthening the 'centre' – or 'powerhouse'. The following few exercises specifically require you to keep your pelvis anchored, abdominals flat, and control of your upper body and limb movement.*

## SINGLE LEG STRETCH

1 Begin on your back with your legs in the tabletop position. Curl your head and chest forward as per the Hundred exercise, then reach your hands toward your ankles. Ensure your hips, back, ribcage and shoulders are stable and prepare your abdominals strongly. Breathe in.

2 As you exhale extend one leg directly away from you at a reasonable height and distance for you to maintain optimal low back stability. Emphasise scooping your abdominals.

3 Breathe in and return your leg to the tabletop position. Focus: shoulders down and stomach in.

4 Exhale, extending your other leg.

5 Inhale, draw the leg back in.

6 Continue to alternate leg extensions for 10-20 repetitions, though rest if you start to lose form.

# OBLIQUE LIFTS

1 Begin on your back with your legs at the tabletop position and your hands behind your head. Ensure pelvis, spine, ribs and shoulders are all stable on the floor and that your elbows are both in your vision. Breathe in and prepare your abdominals.

2 As you exhale, drop your chin gently and roll your shoulders forward, leaning on one side of your ribcage more than the other. (Aim one shoulder to the opposite hip bone.) Don't rotate the body dramatically and keep your hips really still.

3 Inhale as you roll down. Take a brief moment to be stable and keep strong.

4 Exhale, curling up to the other side. Pelvis stable, stomach scooping, ribcage pressing into the floor, shoulder blades stable and flat, chin dropped and both elbows moving in the same direction as your shoulders.

5 Inhale, roll down.

6 Alternate sides, 6-10 repetitions. Maintain a moderate pace and control your breathing.

# ABDOMINAL STRENGTHENING

*(continued)*

# DOUBLE LEG STRETCH

**1** Begin as for the Oblique Lifts, although with your hands placed on your knees. Breathe in, focusing on a strong 'centre.'

**2** Exhale, dropping your chin gently and rolling your chest forward. Reach your arms down by your hips just off the floor. Extend both legs (appropriate to abdominal strength and pelvic/lumbar stability.)

**3** As you inhale, raise your arms to the ceiling without compromising your position.

**4** Exhale, circling your arms sideways so that they then reach back down by your hips. Emphasise your abdominals zipping and shoulder blades flattening.

**5** Breathe in, bend your knees (first) and lie down, bring your legs to tabletop and your hands to your knees. Keep flattening your abdominals as you lie down, because this is essentially your preparation to roll straight back up again.

**6** Repeat 5-10 repetitions.

**NOTE**
Coordinate abdominal strength, breathing, flowing movement and multi-directional manoeuvres.

**MODIFICATION**
While you are gaining abdominal strength and control over the choreography, keep your legs in the tabletop position, or place your feet on a chair or on the floor.

# Spinal Movement & Control

***Purpose*** *Joseph Pilates was quoted as saying that you're as young as your spine is flexible. Fluid, coordinated spinal articulation exercises in various forms help restore moveability to your spine.*

## Pelvic Curl

1 Start in the preparatory position with your arms resting by your sides. Breathe in, feeling the breadth of your back on the floor and an awareness of the pelvic floor and deep abdominals.

2 As you exhale, press the abdominals in toward your spine, rolling your tailbone skyward. Continue to peel your pelvis, and gradually your spine, from the floor. Press both feet equally into the floor to ensure both hips remain symmetrical.

3 Take time to breathe in as you secure the high position. Relax your neck, shoulders and ribcage. Strengthen your ankles, thighs and hips.

4 Exhale, roll down starting from the shoulders. Articulate through the spine, roll through the back of your waist before the hips touch the floor.

5 Repeat 3-5 times.

## PROGRESSION

To challenge the strength of your legs and back, and the stability of your pelvis, lift one foot off the floor while you are at the top of the curl. Do one leg lift each side, without straining the lower back or dropping one hip down, then roll back to the floor. Breathe calmly, one breath for each movement.

## NOTE

While your abdominals secure your lower back, you lift your tail from the floor by means of the hamstring and lower fibres of the gluteal muscles. Imagine the muscles you sit on. Be aware to balance on your shoulder blades and not your neck at the top of the movement.

# SPINAL MOVEMENT & CONTROL

*(continued)*

# SPINAL MOBILITY

**1** Lie on your side with a pillow under your head. Bend your knees and reach your arms directly in front of your chest. Lengthen your spine and retract your shoulder blades gently.

**2** As you inhale, raise your arm to the ceiling without rolling backward. Keep your shoulder blade flat and your neck relaxed.

**3** Exhale, rolling your ribcage, shoulders and head backward while maintaining a long position with your outstretched arm and not allowing the shoulder to collapse toward your neck.

**4** Inhale, stay. You should feel your upper back moving gently and feel associated stretches through the ribcage and chest. Try to keep your shoulder blade flattening down toward your waist.

**5** As you exhale, raise your arm to the ceiling and return to your initial position.

**6** Repeat 3-4 times each side.

# SPINAL MOVEMENT & CONTROL

*(continued)*

## SPINE STRETCH

**1** Start sitting up straight with your legs stretched out in front of you, just wider than your hips. Bend your knees if you need to in order to achieve an ideal straight back posture. Lift your abdominal muscles and drop your shoulders. Inhale.

**2** Exhale, nodding your chin down and slowly rolling your spine down toward the floor in front of you. Try to articulate through each level of your spine to encourage better joint movement throughout. Round 'forward' as far as you are comfortable without slouching back into your pelvis or rolling too far forward off your sitting bones.

**3** Breathe in. Relax your shoulders and expand through the back of your ribcage to breathe. Keep the pelvic floor and abdominals lifted.

**4** As you exhale, emphasise your abdominals lifting up away from the floor and begin rolling your lower back up to neutral. Gradually rebuild your spine to an upright position, relaxing your shoulders as you sit up completely.

**5** Repeat 3-5 times, with an option of remaining in the stretch forward position for two or three full breaths before rolling up. Flexing the ankles at the bottom of the movement will intensify the stretch.

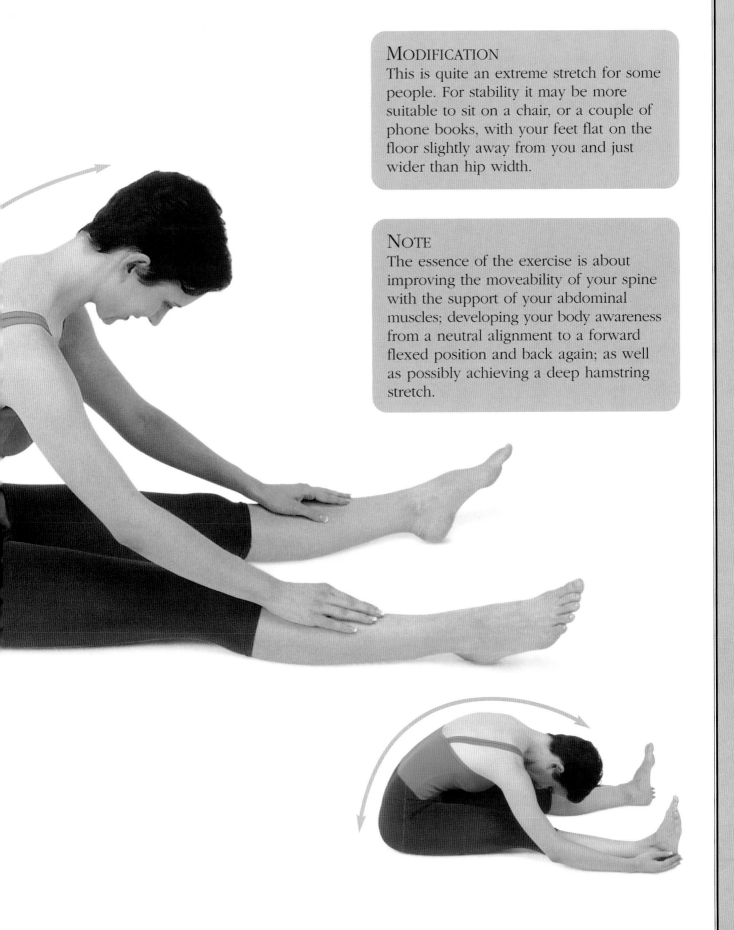

## MODIFICATION

This is quite an extreme stretch for some people. For stability it may be more suitable to sit on a chair, or a couple of phone books, with your feet flat on the floor slightly away from you and just wider than hip width.

## NOTE

The essence of the exercise is about improving the moveability of your spine with the support of your abdominal muscles; developing your body awareness from a neutral alignment to a forward flexed position and back again; as well as possibly achieving a deep hamstring stretch.

# SIDE STABILITY

*Purpose* *While balancing on the smaller surface area of your thigh, ribcage and shoulder, your 'core stabiliser' and hip muscles have to work harder, while you develop the coordination of added leg movement.*

## SIDE LEG LIFTS

1 Lie on your side with both legs straight. (You may need a pillow under your head.) Elongate your spine, keep your abdominals and ribs drawn in and try to make sure that your hip bones are vertically aligned so that your spine is not rotating.

2 Breathe in, lifting your top leg slightly. Don't move your pelvis, lift through your waist muscles and keep both knees straight and pointing forward.

3 As you exhale, lift your underneath leg to join your top leg and lower them both together. Throughout this transition, your pelvis and spine should not move. Press your abdominals in toward your spine especially in preparation to lift the second leg. (Be conscious not to allow the legs to swing behind you.)

4 Repeat 8-10 times, then…

# SIDE STABILITY

*(continued)*

### SIDE LEG LIFTS *(continued)*

**5** Keep your legs together and hover them just off the floor. Emphasise a long, strong waist, maintaining a sensation of a connection between your ribs and hip bones. Lift and lower just your top leg, exhaling every time you draw the legs together. Keep the underneath leg still and reaching out long.

**6** Repeat 5-10 times.

**7** Then, lower and lift your underneath leg, exhaling as you lift it each time. Maintain abdominals and keep an even pace. Keep your top leg still and lengthened.

**8** Repeat 5-10 times.

**9** Repeat ALL on the other side.

# SIDE STABILITY

*(continued)*

> **NOTE**
> This exercise is purely a movement for the top hip joint in order to strengthen the muscles of the outside and back of the hip. Your pelvis needs to remain level and stable all the while, and your abdominal muscles must work significantly to stabilise the trunk. Visualise a straight-backed chair posture.

## SIDE KICK

1 Lie on your side with your underneath leg bent and forward at a right angle. Stretch your top leg directly below you, straight and slightly above hip level. Ensure that your torso is aligned so that your spine does not rotate.

2 As you inhale, flex your ankle and take your top leg forward with a double pulse, only as far as you can maintain an ideal spinal alignment. Keep your knee pointing forward and your leg slightly above hip level.

3 Exhale, point your foot, sweeping your leg straight back without disturbing the position of your pelvis and spine.

4 Repeat 8-10 times, then on the other side.

# SCAPULA STABILITY & BACK STRENGTHENING

***Purpose*** *Shoulder, upper back, abdominal and hip muscles need strength for good posture. The following exercises challenge their endurance in a less stable position.*

## 4 POINT KNEELING SWIMMING

1 Start kneeling on your hands and knees, with your knees under hip joints and hands under shoulder joints. Your spine and head should be in neutral alignment. Engage the deep abdominal and pelvic floor muscles and stabilise your shoulder blades.

2 As you breathe in, slide your opposite hand and foot along the floor and lift them slightly. Try to keep your body still and stable.

3 Exhale, drawing them back to the 4-point position.

4 Repeat with the opposite sides, and continue alternating for 8-10 repetitions.

## NOTE
Having to support some of your body weight with your arms and shoulders forces you to think about the position of your shoulder blades and upper sections of your spine. Try to develop the muscles around your shoulder blades for upper trunk strength and continue to reinforce the abdominal and hip muscles for greater pelvic and lower back stability. Keep your head lifted slightly and your chin gently tucked.

# GLUTE PULSES

**1** Begin kneeling on your hands and knees. Lift through your abdominals and stabilise your shoulders. In a mirror, check the side view, that your spine appears to be quite level as a 'tabletop' is.

**2** Lift one leg backward, and, keeping it bent, pulse with small lifts toward the ceiling. Only lift as far as your spine does not change shape. Exhale with each up movement and ensure that the movement happens from the hip joint and not the knee.

**3** Repeat 10-20 pulses on each leg.

**NOTE**
Ensure shoulders are drawn down, abdominals lift up, hips remain square and your head does not drop too low. Think of lifting your thigh each pulse with the muscles you 'sit on'.

# Scapula Stability & Back Strengthening

*(continued)*

> ### Note
> A full plank position is a true test of full body strength and stability. Only embark on this exercise if your spine is healthy and you are confident with sufficient abdominal and shoulder strength for the support of good spinal alignment.

## PLANK PREP

**1** Still in your 4-point kneeling position, place the heels of your hands forward where the tips of your fingers were, and lean on your hands in this new position, keeping the knees where they were. Tuck your toes under... stabilise your shoulders... lift your abdominals... and engage your glutes – mildly tucking your tail under.

**2** Breathe in, straightening one leg so that you are a straight line from heel to shoulder on that side.

**3** Exhale, straighten your other leg so that you are now in a 'plank', or 'push up', position. Emphasise shoulders down, stomach up and your 'seat' muscles very slightly squeezing under. Stretch your leg muscles long.

**4** Inhale, bend your first knee to kneel again.

**5** Exhale, bend the other knee. Your torso should remain fairly still in space regardless of where your legs are moving.

**6** Repeat 4-6 times, alternating which leg starts first each time.

**7** Repeat 2-4 times, where both legs stretch or bend together – exhaling upon any movement.

# Scapula Stability & Back Strengthening

*(continued)*

## Back Extension with Arms

1 Lie face down, resting your forehead on a rolled towel. Place your arms at 90 degree angles next to your shoulders. Realise where your anchor points are on the floor – your ribcage and your pelvic bones. (You may require a folded towel, or small pillow, under your abdomen to support the lumbar spine.) Draw your abdominal muscles up like a zip action without moving your spine. Inhale.

2 As you exhale, mildly draw your shoulders away from your ears and hover your forehead and chest just off the floor, while you anchor your lower ribcage to the floor.

3 Breathe in, maintaining your shoulder posture, and lift your hands. Keep a strong connection with your abdominals and keep the pubic bone on the floor.

4 Exhale, lower your hands without going 'round' shouldered.

5 Inhale, relax your body down.

6 Repeat 3-6 times.

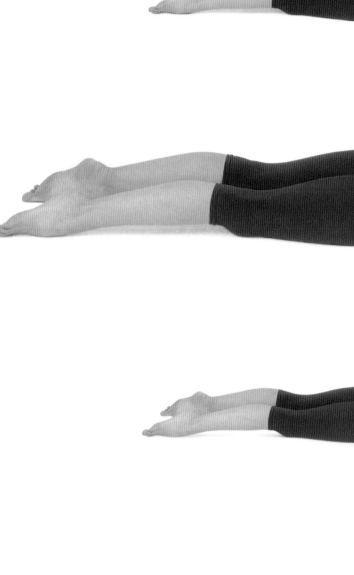

## PROGRESSION

If you have good shoulder movement and a stable lower back, lift your chest, keeping your shoulder blades drawn flat... then lift your hands, then your elbows. Then, elbows down to the floor first, hands down, then chest down. Breathe through the movement... maintain strong abdominals... balance on your ribs... shoulder blades stable and flat... neck tension free... chin tucked mildly and whenever your elbows lift, ensure that your shoulders don't drop and become rounded.

## MODIFICATION

If you find it too difficult to lift your hands, it is probably because you are allowing your shoulders to stay 'rounded' forward. Omit the arm movement and focus on strengthening your upper back without neck strain. Visualise bending backward from the upper thoracic area, much like the image of the Egyptian sphinx. Don't look up – keep your chin slightly down as you lift your chest.

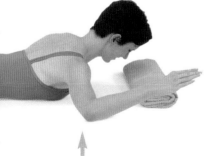

# Scapula Stability & Back Strengthening

*(continued)*

## Caterpillar

1 Kneel on your hands and knees, as for Swimming and Glute Pulses. Inhale.

2 As you exhale, draw your abdominal muscles up and tuck your tail under, curving your lower back. Continue to gradually curl your spine into a round shape allowing your head to drop down at the last.

3 Inhale, expanding your ribs.

4 Exhale, lift your tail bone skyward slightly to allow your lower back to flatten and gradually undulate the spine through to a neutral and mildly extended position, ending with drawing your shoulders down and looking up slightly. Keep your stomach and pelvic floor muscles lifted.

5 Inhale.

6 Repeat 3-4 times in full.

# PELVIC STABILITY & HIP ENDURANCE

***Purpose*** *The ability to move your hip joints without moving your pelvis or lower back will help you achieve greater hip joint mobility, as well as tone the hip and thigh muscles.*

## CUSHION SQUEEZE

1 Start in the preparatory position on your back. Place a cushion between your knees and keep your feet no wider than the width of your sitting bones. Breathe evenly and focus on your abdominals. Inhale.

2 Exhale, squeezing your thighs together without moving your pelvis. Elongate your breaths, so it takes about 4 counts to squeeze.

3 As you inhale, take about 4 counts to release your knees. Maintain your pelvic floor and deep abdominals.

4 Repeat 4-5 times, then again with your legs in the tabletop position, ensuring greater stability throughout the spine and pelvis.

# Clam

**1** Lie on your side with your knees bent and your feet in line with your tail. Don't allow your 'top' hip to roll forward: ensure pelvic alignment and light abdominal bracing. You may require a pillow for your head. Inhale.

**2** Exhale, keeping your heels relaxed together, lift your top knee in an arc motion without moving your pelvis at all.

**3** Inhale as you slowly lower your leg.

**4** Repeat 10-15 times for each leg. Keep a moderate pace to achieve greater hip control and endurance.

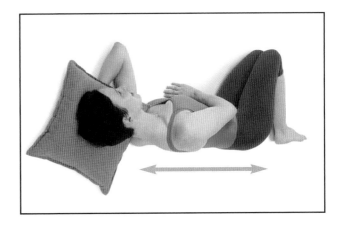

# FULL BODY INTEGRATION

**Purpose** *Ultimately, Pilates exercises are aimed at you being able to integrate all the principles into sequenced movement and mobilise some parts of the body while stabilising the pelvis and shoulder girdle. Teaser and various preparations will challenge your coordination, balance, strength and control.*

## TEASER PREP

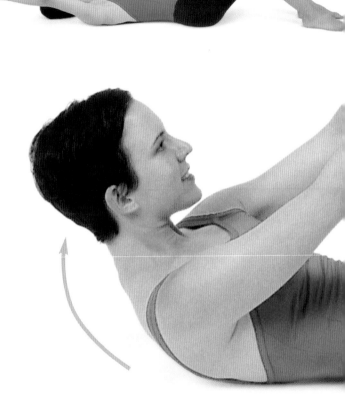

**1** Start on your back with your knees bent. Reach your arms overhead and ensure that your abdominals are braced, that your ribs are flat on the floor and that your shoulders are drawing down.

**2** As you breathe in reach both arms to the ceiling and deepen the bracing action of your abdominals.

**3** Exhale as you nod your chin and roll your spine off the floor until you are balancing on the back of your pelvis. Reach your arms forward and keep your legs still.

**4** Breathe in as you lengthen your torso on a slight incline away from your thighs. Imagine your tail as an anchor on the floor. Lift and press your abdominals firmly to your spine and raise your arms to challenge your strength.

**5** Exhale. Emphasise rolling through your lower back. Control the spinal articulation back to the floor and finish reaching both arms overhead. Repeat 3-5 times, aiming for optimal movement control and flow.

Teaser has a different feeling to a Roll Up in that you need to 'feel' the resistance of yourself rolling more on an 'uphill incline' angle. The use of gravity is different (although both exercises require you to have a strongly anchored pelvis and use your legs as levers.) Ensure that your priority is always the 'rolling' action of your spine – particularly that of your lumbar and lower thoracic – in keeping with optimal control of the deep abdominal muscles.

# STRETCHES

***Purpose*** *The following stretches target some key areas that are generally prone to tightness. Take care to stretch within your range of comfort. Improving or maintaining your suppleness is just as important as muscle strengthening.*

## HIP FLEXOR, PSOAS & HAMSTRING STRETCH

1 Begin kneeling on one knee with your other leg bent in front of you. Legs should be parallel, with the majority of your body weight on your back knee. Tuck your tail under and transfer your weight onto your front foot slightly...in order to facilitate a stretch at the front of your (kneeling) hip. Don't allow your lower back to arch or your hips to twist to the side. Breathe through the stretch.

2 Lunge forward and place your hands either side of your front foot. Take your body weight onto your hands, the front thigh and foot. Allow your back leg to relax so that the front of the hip stretches. Continue to breathe.

3 Take your full body weight onto the front foot and stand on the back foot, straightening both legs, keeping one forward and one back (depending on your flexibility). Both feet should point forward and your priority is keeping your hips square. You can bend one or both knees slightly to achieve the hamstring stretch with good pelvic alignment. Relax your head, neck and shoulders. Breathe.

4 Repeat all stretches on the other side, holding each one for between 30-90 seconds.

# STRETCHES

*(continued)*

## ADDUCTOR STRETCH & FROG

**1** Sit on the floor and extend one leg out to the side, as far as you can keeping both hip bones square to the front. Keep your other leg bent in front of you. Lean forward carefully and take your body weight onto your arms if you can. Depending on your hip joint range and flexibility, you may be more comfortable on a couple of phone books or even on the edge of a bench/table. Ensure the knee of your outstretched leg points up to the ceiling. Breathe.

**2** Repeat on the other leg.

**3** Still sitting, bring the soles of your feet together and allow your knees to open out to the sides. Depending on your hip range you may feel this stretch in the inner or outer hip/thigh. Breathe.

# STRETCHES

*(continued)*

## MERMAID

**1** Sitting cross-legged on the floor (if comfortable, otherwise sit on the edge of a bench/table with your legs together) lengthen your spine and raise one arm, leaving your other hand near the floor close to your knee.

**2** Carefully bend sideways towards the low arm for a side stretch on the opposite side. Use your abdominal muscles and allow your head and neck to relax as you lean on your bottom arm. Breathe, and when returning to a straight spine, engage the abdominals and slowly return as you exhale.

**3** Repeat 1-3 times each side. You may alternate.

### MODIFICATION
You may need something higher to lean on if it is difficult to stretch this far. Be cautious of this stretch if you have lower back pain.

# GLOSSARY

### ABDOMINALS
Common term for the group of abdominal muscles. The 'six-pack' crunches you forward, the obliques (waist muscles) rotate and twist your trunk, and the deep layer of abdominal muscle (transversus abdominus) works to stabilise your spine against any of the actions just noted.

### ADDUCTORS
Muscles of the inner thighs, which draw one leg toward the other.

### GLUTES
The gluteal group of muscles are those of the buttocks, which contribute to hip movement and stability of the pelvis and lower back.

### HAMSTRINGS
The group of muscles at the back of the thigh running from the sitting bone to the back of the knee joint. These assist in backward leg motion and bending of the knee.

### HIP FLEXORS
Muscles of the front of the hip (groin area), one of which is the psoas. They act to lift the thigh toward the torso.

### LUMBAR SPINE
The five vertebrae that form the lower back region, above the pelvis.

### PELVIC FLOOR
A thin layering of muscles suspended across the pelvic girdle. It supports the weight of the abdominal organs and shares nerve connection with the respiratory diaphragm and deep abdominal muscles. Activation of the pelvic floor therefore assists in stabilising the lower back and contributes to the strengthening of the deep abdominal muscles. This is important for improving your posture.

### SCAPULA
The shoulder blade, which helps make up the shoulder joint and provides attachments for most of the muscles of the upper back. Stabilising the scapulae so that they are flat against the back of the ribcage is essential for good posture.

### THORACIC SPINE
The twelve vertebrae that form the upper and middle back. These vertebrae also provide attachment sites for the ribs. (Note: the cervical spine is that of the neck; the sacrum and coccyx make up the most lower part of the spine).

# CONCLUSION

When you practise Pilates with purpose and consistency, you will achieve freedom of movement, improved sense of centre and balance, and greater levels of energy. The aim is to provide you with a flexible, more supple body. With regular practice, improvements in your physical ability will also become apparent. Remember that your goal is to coordinate your breathing, correct abdominal bracing, pelvic and lumbar stability and the release of unnecessary strain.

Mastering the 'choreography' of the exercises is of course necessary for the development of all the Pilates principles. However this must remain a secondary objective - 'quality over quantity' is what you require. Focus your mind, keep a moderate pace and keep reminding yourself of the principles behind the movement. This will allow you to gain the most benefit from *More Simply Pilates*.

*More Simply Pilates* is an all rounded home workout program designed for you to enhance your fitness regime. For greater benefit from your practise of Pilates, or if you require assistance with your comprehension of this unique exercise philosophy, visit a reputable Pilates studio.

# SIMPLY
# PILATES

— WITH —

## STRETCHBAND

Author: Jennifer Pohlman
Art Director: Karen Moores
Editor: Jane Keighley
Graphic Artist: Susie Allen
Photographer: Paul Broben
Assistant Co-ordinator: Rodney Searle

# CONTENTS

# INTRODUCTION

In the early 1900s, German-born Joseph Pilates devised a system of movement which, when practised regularly focusing on quality of movement and alignment, will give you improved general fitness.

Pilates, in its true form, is a training regime based on the principles of refining physical motion. This exercise regime is gentle, effective and often subtle, requiring patience and consistency in order to achieve long-term benefits. The exercises were designed to be performed with exact technique and minimal repetitions, encompassing the less-is-more workout philosophy.

Joseph educated his students to be dedicated to the discipline on a daily basis, so mind and body were conditioned and the movement (much like martial arts or dance) was worked to perfection.

Joseph died in the 1960s but his exercise method evolved into various forms, with his original students dispersing to cities all over the world to establish their own training schools. Although the Pilates Method of body conditioning can vary greatly in 'what' it is and 'how' it is taught around the globe, the Pilates principles, which are the philosophy behind Joseph's exercises, are the common thread that binds the different Pilates schools. Physical therapists use the basis of Pilates postural concepts, along with modified versions of the movement sequences, for rehabilitating patients and the elderly.

At the other end of the spectrum, Pilates floor classes are becoming commonplace in gyms and fitness centres, varying by degrees of difficulty and dynamics. There are now an increasing number of Pilates exercise studios, predominantly in main cities, which host private and semi-private sessions so you can experience a full-body workout program using a combination of floor and equipment exercises.

Joseph originally developed the repertoire of floor exercises for the purpose of full-body conditioning, then later improvised with springs and pulleys to take the method to another level – inventing Pilates equipment. Integrating a stretchband into a Pilates floor workout can simulate resistance that is usually achieved on Pilates equipment.

His own exercise studio was situated in the same building as a major ballet company in New York City and he worked with the dancers to correct muscle imbalances, improve symmetry and eradicate poor movement patterns. He referred to his exercise system as The Art of Contrology and endeavoured to help people from all walks of life. Although he had devised choreographed movements for the purpose of full-body strengthening, he believed it was the principles with which his students executed the movements that were essential.

# PILATES PRINCIPLES

Joseph's knowledge and experience of physical movement helped him devise a fusion of principles that epitomise a sensible approach to training the body for greater proficiency of movement. He believed an individual could train their body to perfect their daily movement patterns, whether they are an office worker or an athlete. If you embody these following powerful fundamentals, you will achieve the most from practising the Pilates technique:

- **Concentration** – visualisation and mental focus are essential to gain muscle control
- **Control** – quality movement is most beneficial and less harmful to joints and muscles
- **Centring** – the abdomen, lower back, hips and buttocks comprise the 'powerhouse' – the primary focus for strength, stability and 'core' control
- **Fluidity** – graceful, flowing motion is required, with no static, abrupt or rushed movements
- **Precision** – purposeful movement and good body alignment develops better muscle patterns for everyday activities
- **Breathing** – calm, rhythmic breathing assists muscle control and energises the whole system

Joseph was influenced by various physical disciplines, such as body building, boxing, diving, gymnastics and dance. Of course, these exacting sports require ultimate physical conditioning. They depend on strength, suppleness, control, precision, agility and the acquired understanding of movement quality and dynamics. Training the body for specific sporting manoeuvres requires consistent practise, allowing the individual to develop strength and efficiency in what

it is they need to do repetitively. Considering the extreme fitness usually required for such sports, it was apparent to Joseph how certain physical laws, or principles, needed to be followed in order to make the process possible. Fusing concepts of strength building with holistic life philosophies of Eastern origins, the principles aim to help people manage and improve their physical limitations. He developed a series of choreographed movements and personally instructed individuals through tailored training sessions ranging from gentle to rigorous exercise sequences. Not unlike an athlete training his body to execute movement

# PILATES EQUIPMENT

with proficiency, the average person needs to ensure their body is fit for general living. Everyday movement – for example, carrying a washing basket full of wet clothes, climbing stairs repetitively, sustaining reasonable posture in front of a computer, maintaining spinal strength and stability while growing slowly while pregnant – all require a certain level of strength and endurance training. Everybody needs to develop and maintain optimal physical fitness for general living as well as any particular repetitive tasks they need to perform, to ensure their muscles and joints stay as resilient to wear and tear as possible. One-sided activities have an impact on our spines. Nursing a child on one hip, swinging a golf club and even driving a manual car creates muscular imbalance in our bodies. We need to condition our body to suit our needs. Pilates is a perfect body conditioning method for almost everybody to re-create muscle symmetry and strength.

It was essential to Joseph that the principles behind his Method were the central focus of each exercise, and when equipment was introduced it was an aid to challenge, modify or help facilitate movement which was otherwise not possible. He was adamant about the individual being in total control of their trunk and limbs. Appropriate muscle control needs to be used with, and against, the resistance of the springs. At no moment is the source of resistance to execute the movement for the individual. It is not about what a particular piece of equipment does for the body, but rather how an individual can achieve their optimum with the use of the equipment.

In a fully equipped Pilates studio, the equipment available to today's instructors is very close to that of Joseph's specially designed, spring-resistance based tables and carriages (on wheels, with pulleys and straps). A modern Pilates studio, which bases its teachings on Joseph's original work, can comprise of various exercise apparatus, as well as smaller pieces of equipment to challenge or assist the individual in their exercises. It is the above mentioned spring-loaded equipment that can be duplicated in effort and movement sequences on the mat with a stretchband.

# THE BENEFITS

Pilates principles are very adaptable to different mediums, which is why many medical and fitness professionals recognise the benefits of incorporating it into people's daily lives. Depending on an individual's fitness, co-ordination and musculoskeletal complications, anybody can perform Pilates exercises to some level and experience many different benefits. Due to the adaptability of Pilates, it is almost impossible to describe to someone who has not yet experienced its benefits, what it is.

Pilates is arguably of most benefit when taught individually to a person, or at most, up to four people at a time. The reason is that all bodies are unique – with different strengths and weaknesses – and Pilates exercises can be modified for you to achieve the most positive muscle patterning. This allows you to gradually build up to achieving a secure execution of pure Pilates sequencing. This process is fundamental when beginning Pilates, to prevent the development of bad habits in movement and to improve existing poor postural and movement habits.

Pilates is simply a sensible and correct method of physical realignment and strengthening – a fact well proven and documented through testimonials over the last 80–90 years. These include people devoted to practising Pilates for numerous reasons – general fitness, improved wellbeing, pain management, injury prevention, rehabilitation and post-natally, among others. From the athlete who uses Pilates to complement their other training, to the office worker who usually loathes exercise, regular Pilates sessions are a refreshing way to clear your mind and effectively strengthen and tone the body. The movement sequences are never boring and can increase in difficulty or intensity as you gain strength and perspective of the Method. Pilates can be many things and many ways of moving: it can become part of your lifestyle as it enhances your total wellbeing and improves your quality of living.

# PRACTICAL MATTERS

Joseph was an advocate of the less-is-more philosophy when it came to exercise. In other words, the body is not forced or overworked to gain strength and endurance. In today's society of instant gratification, the masses are keen for any new fitness fad. Pilates, having the notable reputation for moulding sleek, strong physiques, is certainly no exception. However, there is a trade-off: commitment to routine practise and being very intuitive with your own body – taking it step-by-step and building on your physical successes with realistic progressions. Each exercise requires specific attention to detail – of both your alignment and your purpose of movement (i.e. what are you strengthening?).

Pilates is multi-functional as you introduce it to your fitness regime. Aiming for daily practise is ideal, even if it is only 15–20 minutes. Or realistically, schedule your practice sessions around your week's commitments and other sensible exercise. Pilates is a perfect addition to cross-training regimes.

Note: If you have a history of spinal, hip or shoulder problems, or if you are pregnant, seek advice from your medical practioner or visit a reputable Pilates studio prior to commencing these exercises.

## REQUIREMENTS

During your Pilates floor workout, the mat or carpet surface you lie on must be comfortable. However, if it is too soft, you will find it too difficult to maintain the natural curvature of your spine and your body will be forced to recruit other muscles to create a sense of stability. Your neck and shoulders must remain tension-free, so a small pillow or book may be required under your head. A low chair or a couple of phone books will create an appropriate height for you to sit on during the seated exercises if your hips and back lack the suppleness to sit completely upright. This is important when doing exercises that are specifically about correcting your posture. A cushion and bath-sized towel may be of assistance to you if your back or neck is compromised during any of the exercises. These options are explained in the content of the book.

# CENTRING & BREATHING

The following three concepts are fundamental to developing good posture. Awareness of these concepts should be a prerequisite to any Pilates workout, and will ensure that you obtain maximum benefit from the exercises.

## BREATHING

Taking a moment to meditate on the rhythm of your breathing can be relaxing, release muscle tension, energise your whole system and ultimately draw your attention to your abdominal muscles. Take time to focus on how you breathe. Allow your ribs to soften and expand (side and back) as you breathe in, and merely relax as you exhale. In Pilates, we term this lateral breathing. The breathing exercise in this book will instruct you in co-ordinating breath and abdominal control. Over time this will feel fairly easy, allowing you to execute the Pilates exercises with greater ease and confidence.

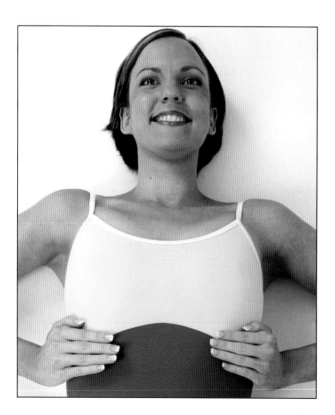

## NEUTRAL PELVIS

This is the most ideal position for you to strengthen your deep abdominal muscles in order to maintain or improve the stability of your spine. Lie on your back and relax your hip muscles. Usually the hip bones (iliac crests) and the pubic bone all form a parallel level with the floor. Maintaining a neutral position of the pelvis will automatically position the spine in its natural alignment. Before and throughout the exercises, the pelvis and spine must be stable in neutral, unless you are specifically rolling or mobilising your spine.

When your legs are in a tabletop (refer to page 153) position – as described in Hundred (refer to page 157), for instance – your pelvis should remain in neutral alignment with a *feeling* of anchoring your spine to the floor. The key is developing the abdominal and back strength to maintain this position. Don't forcefully push your lower back into the floor as this will cause you to overwork muscles unnecessarily.

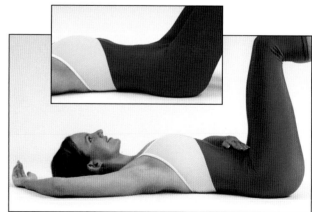

# ABDOMINAL PATTERNING

Relaxed on your back is possibly the easiest position in which to establish awareness of correct abdominal activation. Place your hands on your lower abdomen and breathe normally. With your hips totally relaxed and maintaining your neutral pelvis and spine, merely sink or draw your abdomen away from your hands. The main thing to avoid is over-trying – never grip or clench your muscles. Subtleness is essential in creating an awareness of your deeper abdominal muscles. Your spine does not move, but try to visualise your belly and waist shrinking or being drawn in towards the front side of the spinal column itself. Because our deep postural muscles share nerve connections, lifting your pelvic floor muscles (while keeping your hips and buttocks relaxed) may assist in developing an intrinsic awareness of strengthening your core.

### PREPARATORY NOTE

Pilates exercises – as well as associated modifications – require you to fuse the technical concepts of centring and breathing with general commonsense good posture. Know that the position of your head will affect your neck alignment. When you are lying on your back, your forehead and chin should be in a line parallel to the floor and your neck muscles should be free of tension. Place any pillow you may need under your head, not your neck. Remember, if you have pain or discomfort starting any of these exercises, discontinue and seek advice from a qualified professional.

During the execution of many Pilates exercises, you will be required to intensify this abdominal action, as well as squeeze your gluteal muscles (buttocks) a little. Take care not to bunch, or clench your abdominals in this case. Always aim for a flattening, scooping sensation with the abdomen while maintaining your neutral position.

# Centring & Breathing *(continued)*

## Breathing Exercise

**1** Lie on your back with your knees bent at a 90 degree angle, feet opposite your sitting bones (refer to page 191) and arms comfortably by your sides. This will be referred to as the preparatory position, because when you lie on your back, it is the simplest way of drawing your attention to full-body alignment.

**2** Assume a normal breathing pattern and be aware of maintaining your neutral pelvis position.

**3** Keeping your neck and shoulders tension free and your hips totally relaxed, focus on your abdominal muscles gently bracing, or scooping. While you breathe, maintain the deep lower abdominal action without any spinal movement.

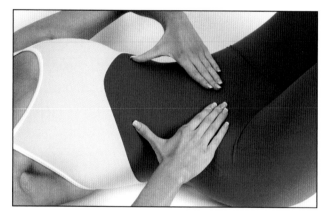

**4** This concept can be practised while sitting. Wrap the stretchband around your ribcage so that you can have an immediate sensation of your ribs expanding and relaxing while you breathe. This may actually be very useful in creating awareness of your abdominal muscles engaging while you breathe freely.

### Note
Visualisation techniques are often useful during Pilates exercises. Try imagining that your abdominal muscles are like a deep internal zip beginning near your pubic bone and going up the front of your spine towards your ribcage. Scoop, lift, zip, navel to spine, shrink, press down, draw in, inward and upward are all Pilates talk to help you visualise the action of your abdominal muscles for strengthening and stabilising purposes.

# Scapula Movement

1 Lie on your back with the stretchband under your shoulder blades. Wrap it around the sides of your ribcage so you can hold the ends and reach your arms to the ceiling. While in the preparatory position, remember to focus on your breathing and abdominal technique. Relax your neck and shoulders.

2 As you inhale, push the stretchband towards the ceiling allowing your shoulder blades to move with your arms. Try to keep your ribcage, neck and head still and fairly relaxed.

3 Exhale using the muscles of your armpits and upper back to draw your shoulder blades back to their correct, flat alignment. Only move your shoulder blades enough to feel that you are creating a V formation with your back muscles. Keep your ribcage, neck and head still.

4 Repeat 5–6 times.

## Note
Don't squeeze your shoulder blades together. Simply replace them to where you would consider them to be your best posture.

# POSTURE AWARENESS

**Purpose:** *To mobilise and stretch your shoulders without straining your neck or moving your spine. These basic movements are preparatory exercises while you focus on the concepts of Centring & Breathing.*

## ARM OPENINGS

**1** Keep the stretchband under your upper back. Stay in the preparatory position and begin with your arms up towards the ceiling. Remember to breathe calmly and continue training your lower abdominals to gently shrink down towards the floor.

**2** As you inhale, open your arms to the sides while you maintain correct alignment of the torso.

**3** Exhale as you close your arms again. Relax your neck and keep your focus on your abdominal action and your shoulder blades being flat and stable.

**4** Repeat 5–10 times.

# LAT STRETCH

**1** Lie in the preparatory position and reach your arms towards the ceiling, holding the stretchband as though it was a pole. Breathe evenly and shrink through your stomach.

**2** As you exhale, float your arms back to the floor behind you. Don't allow your ribs to arch off the floor. Maintain strong abdominal muscles as you lengthen your arms away from your ribcage.

**3** Inhale as your arms return. Keep your shoulder blades flat and stable and relax your neck.

**4** Repeat 5–6 times.

# POSTURE AWARENESS *(continued)*

## PEC RELEASE

**1** Stay in the preparatory position and keep the stretchband in your hands as though it was a pole. Bend your arms and rest them on the floor, placing the band above your head – taut but not stretched. Maintain your focus on ribcage and shoulder alignment so you don't compromise your neck, back or shoulder joints.

**2** As you inhale, slide your arms along the floor further away from your head. Keep the distance between your hands about the same as the width of your elbows. There is no need to achieve straight arms because the purpose is to mobilise your shoulder joints while you maintain torso stability, and to keep your neck free of tension.

**3** Exhale, bending your arms as they slide back towards you. You will possibly feel a stretch at the front of your shoulders and into your chest. Regardless, focus on the muscles of your upper back and stomach while you relax your neck and chest. Find a balance between not allowing your ribs to arch from the floor and maintaining a correct abdominal bracing action.

**4** Repeat 5–6 times. Remember that the movement does not have to be big.

## NOTE

If this position is not achievable for your shoulders, upper back and neck, place your hands on your shoulders and let your arms relax out to the sides. Or stretch your arms out to the sides in a long position as far as comfortable to allow some stretch to occur across your chest and shoulders. Your neck should not experience any discomfort, your head should not be tilting backwards or your shoulders shrugging up towards your ears. If you are comfortable allow the stretch to continue for up to 1 minute.

# WARM UP

***Purpose:*** *To integrate the concepts of better posture into exercises that begin to challenge your co-ordination as well as gently mobilise your spine. This will prepare your body for subsequent exercises.*

# PELVIC CURL

**1** Lie in the preparatory position with the stretchband around your shins, holding onto the ends with some resistance. Engage your deep abdominals. Inhale.

**2** As you exhale, scoop your abdominals towards your lower back and curl your tailbone towards the ceiling. Peel your spine from the floor as if you are moving one vertebrae at a time. The stretchband may be slightly taut, reminding you of your shoulder posture. Relax your neck.

**3** While at the peak of the lifted position, ensure it is your seat muscles (lower gluteals and hamstrings) lifting you and not your lower back. Breathe in laterally through your ribcage. Maintain tight abdominals and relax your neck.

**4** As you exhale, reverse the roll gently as if you're imprinting the image of your spine, ribs and pelvis on the floor. Relax your hips completely at the end but maintain zipped abdominals.

**5** Repeat 4–6 times.

# WARM UP *(continued)*

## CHEST LIFT

**1** Start in the preparatory position and rest your head in the stretchband so that you can relax your neck muscles. Keep your focus on your shoulder blade stability, breathing and abdominal pattern. Don't allow your elbows to be too wide and keep your chin gently tilting down. Inhale.

**2** As you exhale, roll your head and shoulders forward, flattening your abdominal muscles without moving your hips. Ensure the movement occurs through your ribcage and not through your neck or lower back.

**3** Breathe in while you maintain a strong, broad abdominal bracing action.

**4** Breathe out as you roll back to the floor. Take care not to release or clench your abdominal muscles.

**5** Repeat 5–10 times.

**6** Repeat remaining in the curled position while you continue to breathe. Take 5–10 full calm breaths while you focus on strong abdominals, relaxed thighs, stable shoulders and easy head and neck posture.

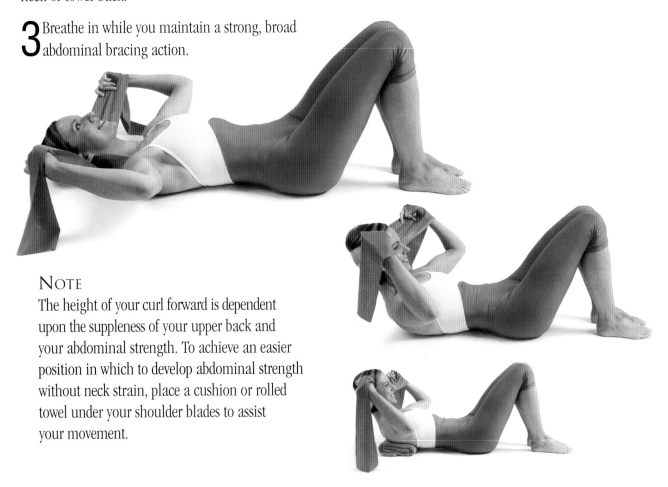

### NOTE
The height of your curl forward is dependent upon the suppleness of your upper back and your abdominal strength. To achieve an easier position in which to develop abdominal strength without neck strain, place a cushion or rolled towel under your shoulder blades to assist your movement.

# Roll Up Prep

**1** Sit with your legs bent in front of you. Keeping your feet flexed and about a tennis ball width apart, place the stretchband around the tops of your feet (toe and ball) and hold the stretchband with some resistance. Sit with fairly tall posture, but not rigid. Inhale.

**2** As you exhale, gently roll your pelvis under so that your lower back becomes rounded. Roll away from your legs ensuring that your deep abdominal muscles pull in towards your spine.

**3** Stop. Inhale. Maintain a deep scoop-up action with your lower abdominal muscles.

**4** Remain still as you exhale – further deepening your abdominal scoop. Be careful not to collapse into your spine. Try to relax your neck and arms. Rather than overworking your shoulders, allow the stretchband to take some of your weight.

**5** Inhale as you roll forward.

**6** Repeat 4–6 times.

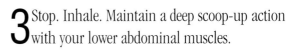

# WARM UP *(continued)*

# FOOTWORK

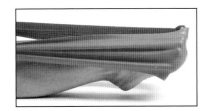

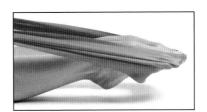

**1** Sit tall with your legs stretched out in front of you, slightly apart, and the stretchband around your toes and balls of your feet. Hold the ends of the stretchband with some resistance. Breathe normally.

**2** Stretch your legs completely and point your feet by way of moving your ankles first and then elongating the ends of your feet, through to the toes (metatarsals). Keep lengthening up through your lower back and stomach. Relax your neck and shoulders.

**3** Flex your feet back up towards the ceiling beginning with your toes first, then your whole foot.

**4** Repeat 10–20 times, depending on the strength and mobility of your feet, ankles and calves.

**5** Maintain a lengthened ankle position and repeat just the metatarsal (toes and balls of your feet) movement for strengthening the underneath surface of your forefoot. Repeat 10–20 times.

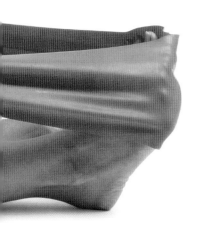

## NOTE

This is the first exercise in your workout where you are sitting tall for a sustained period of time. Ensure you are sitting on your sitting bones, scooping up your abdominal muscles, and keeping your chest open so you can feel your postural muscles strengthen. Remember to sit on something higher if you are struggling to sit completely upright whilst on the floor.

# PELVIC & SPINAL STABILITY

***Purpose:*** *To realise how your core abdominal, hip and back muscles must work in order to keep your spine and pelvis in a natural alignment while your limbs move independently of your torso. This is essential to understand before embarking on traditional Pilates mat work.*

## BEND & STRETCH

**1** Lie in the preparatory position with the stretchband around the ball of one foot. Hold the ends with some resistance and place your elbows on the floor beside you. Ensure you maintain a neutral pelvis, stable ribcage and shoulder blades and shrink through your abdominals.

**2** Exhale as you extend your knee, reaching your leg away from your torso. Maintain correct torso alignment and try not to involve your other leg.

**3** Inhale as you bend your knee and return your leg to a tabletop position.

**4** Repeat 5–10 times.

**5** Keep the same foot in the stretchband and raise your other leg to tabletop, keeping your spine and pelvis stable and correctly flattening your abdominal muscles. Repeat the same exercise as you did with one leg extending in the stretchband. Your abdominal and hip muscles are challenged more since you have no feet on the floor. Keep your tabletop leg still, abdominals scooping, shoulders and ribcage stable, and breathe calmly.

**6** Repeat 5–10 times.

**7** Keep both legs in the tabletop position then extend one leg away from you, maintaining torso stability. Now, as one leg stretches, the other will bend and vice versa. Continue switching your legs while you focus on correct abdominals, breathing and leg alignment. Keep your knees a couple of inches apart and use your thigh and hip muscles.

**8** Repeat 5–10 times.

**9** Repeat all 3 variations with the stretchband around your other foot.

## NOTE

The term tabletop refers to when one or both legs are in the air and bent at a 90 degree angle at both the hip and knee joints. The exact angle of this position will possibly vary between individuals according to your ability to stabilise your back with a secure abdominal pattern. The weight of your legs should be distributed down into your hip joints, or over your hip bones. You should feel no strain, but still keep the abdominal challenge reasonable.

If you struggle with the tabletop position, or cannot stop from clenching or bulging up your abdominal muscles, keep your feet on the floor or rest your feet on a chair until you are strong enough.

# PELVIC &
# SPINAL STABILITY *(continued)*

# DEAD BUG

**1** Begin in the preparatory position and hold the stretchband in both hands as though it was a pole. There is no need to create much resistance with the stretchband as this is just a guide for you to feel how symmetrical your neck, shoulder and ribcage areas are. Reach your arms to the ceiling and flatten your shoulder blades against the floor, relaxing your neck. Scoop and shrink your stomach towards the floor while maintaining a neutral pelvis. Lift one leg to tabletop.

**2** As you breathe out, extend your leg from tabletop away from you and lower your arms towards the floor behind you. Only reach your limbs as far as you can so as to maintain correct torso alignment and stability.

**3** Inhale, returning to the starting position.

**4** Repeat 5–10 times, then swap legs and repeat.

# PILATES FUNDAMENTALS

***Purpose:*** *These exercises were traditionally the first exercises executed in a basic Pilates mat work sequence in order to prepare your body for subsequent abdominal work. Using a stretchband helps you achieve a better abdominal pattern and ensure smooth movement.*

## HUNDRED

**1** Lie on your back with your legs together in the tabletop position. Place the stretchband across your knees or shins and hold the ends in your hands by the sides of your hips.

**2** Exhale as you curl your head and shoulders forward, similar to a Chest Lift position. Maintain correct abdominals, neutral pelvis and breathe calmly and smoothly as you begin pulsing your arms with small, quick movements.

**3** Continue focusing on shrinking your waist and deep abdominal muscles, anchoring your pelvis still and flattening your shoulder blades while you aim for 10 full breaths.

**4** Hold your arms still on your last breath in. Keep your centre strong and still.

**5** Exhale as you rest.

## NOTE
Ultimately, the Hundred exercise should entail the co-ordination of 5 arm pulses each inhale and 5 pulses each exhale. This is to encourage optimal lung capacity while challenging the endurance of your abdominal muscles. So that you don't hyperventilate, start with less pulses per breath and build on that as you gain control and co-ordination.

# PILATES FUNDAMENTALS *(continued)*

## ROLL UP

**1** Sit with your legs bent in front of you, slightly apart, and the stretchband around the balls of your feet. Hold the stretchband relatively loosely, sit tall through your waist and lift your abdominals. Inhale.

**2** As you exhale pull your lower abdominal muscles in towards your spine so that you roll easily backwards. Gradually roll to the floor as though you are gently kneading each section of your spine into the mat. You must feel anchored to the floor by your buttocks so you can move fluidly through your spine.

**3** While you lie on the floor breathe in, focusing on the stability and symmetry of your torso. Keep your deep abdominal muscles engaged inward and upward towards your lower back.

**4** As you exhale, nod your chin gently and roll towards your legs as though you are peeling yourself off the floor. Remember to anchor your hips to the floor and emphasise your abdominals into your lower back to ensure that you roll properly, using your legs as little as possible.

**5** Repeat 3–4 times, then again with straight legs.

### NOTE
While you are learning to articulate your spine and roll properly through your lower back with abdominal control, bent knees are likely to be more suitable to ensure the safety of your spine. Remember also that the stretchband is like training wheels for you to successfully roll up and down with a sense of length, strength and control throughout your spine and abdominal muscles.

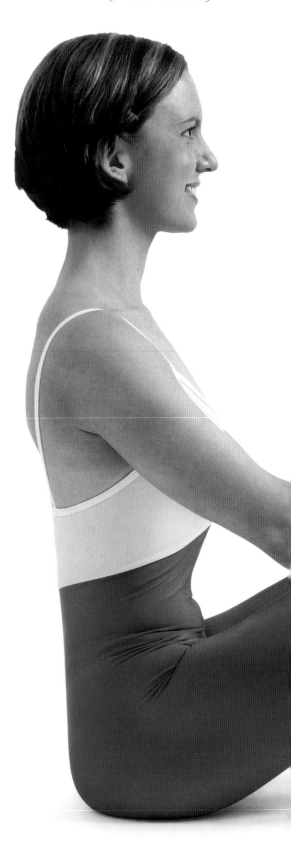

## LEG CIRCLES

**1** Lie on your back with the stretchband around one foot and the other leg either bent or straight on the floor. Hold the ends of the stretchband with some resistance and place your elbows on the floor beside you. Maintain a neutral and well-anchored spine and pelvis. Lengthen your (stretchband) leg towards the ceiling, maintaining correct torso placement. Don't allow your knees to turn in or out – they must line up with your ears or shoulders.

**2** Draw a circle in the air with your foot. Your whole leg should move as this is an exercise to mobilise your hip joint while you keep your pelvis still and abdominals strong. Start your circles across your body first (towards your other hip) and exhale each time your leg raises back towards your body.

**3** Repeat 6–10 times, then reverse the direction. Repeat both directions with your other leg.

## NOTE

Feel your hip, abdominal and upper back muscles bracing to keep your body still and strong while you execute your circles. Lengthen your other leg along the floor to assist you in being stable. Remember to only make the circles as big as you can and keep your torso still. Bend your raised leg if you are struggling to maintain a neutral pelvis.

# PILATES FUNDAMENTALS *(continued)*

## ROLLING PREP

**1** Sit with your legs bent and very close to your body. Your feet should be together, but not necessarily your knees. Hold the stretchband out in front of your legs as though it was a pole. Don't stretch it greatly. Focus, instead, on a rounded body while drawing your shoulder blades flat and keeping your abdominals scooped strongly.

**2** As you exhale, pull your deep abdominal muscles in towards your lower back, causing your hip bones to roll very slightly away from your thighs.

**3** As you inhale, relax.

**4** Repeat 5–6 times.

**5** Repeat again with the stretchband across the front of your thighs. As you draw your stomach away from your thighs, pull the stretchband towards your feet to create an opposing resistance.

In this exercise it is essential to move with subtlety
and focus on releasing your thigh muscles as you
engage your very deep lower abdominal muscles.
There should barely be any movement as this is
merely a preparatory exercise for rolling your spine
on the floor and maintaining a round back. You
are actually refining how you use your abdominal
muscles to flex your spine into a round shape.
If you find your hip muscles are cramping and
you're struggling with your lower back, sit up
on a couple of books.

# INTERMEDIATE ABDOMINALS

***Purpose:*** *To further challenge your abdominal strength and endurance as you become secure with the Pilates warm up and fundamental exercises. While aiming for fluid, co-ordinated movements, you must always emphasise the placement, symmetry and stability of your pelvis, spine, ribcage and shoulder blades.*

## SINGLE LEG STRETCH

**1** Lie on your back with your legs at tabletop and your head and shoulders curled forward. Hold the stretchband like a pole, reach your arms to the ceiling above your waist and flatten your shoulder blades and abdominals. A neutral and anchored pelvis is essential.

**2** Breathe out as you extend one leg away from you and inhale as it returns.

**3** Repeat 10–20 times, alternating legs.

### NOTE
Breathe broadly, ensuring you are flexing forward from the base of your ribcage, flattening your shoulder blades and pressing your lower abdominal muscles deep towards the floor. Do not move your body during the leg extensions.

# CRISS-CROSS

**1** Begin as for Single Leg Stretch.

**2** As you exhale, rotate your upper body and extend your opposite leg.

**3** Inhale and return to centre (stay curled forward) and draw your leg back towards you.

**4** Exhale as you repeat on the other side.

**5** Repeat 8–10 times, alternating sides.

## NOTE
Ensure you only rotate your ribcage as far as you don't lose the flexed forward strength. Your pelvis should remain neutral and anchored still throughout, and your abdominal muscles should be pressing towards your spine constantly.

## DOUBLE LEG STRETCH

**1** Lie on your back with the stretchband around both feet. Don't allow your legs to relax. Keep your feet slightly apart so that you engage your hip muscles. Hold the ends of the stretchband and place your elbows at your sides. Start with a neutral spine and pelvis and your legs at tabletop.

**2** Brace through your deep abdominals and, as you exhale, stretch your legs up and away from your torso. Only go as far as you can, maintaining correct alignment and abdominal work.

**3** Inhale as your legs return. Maintain flat abdominals and stable ribs and shoulder blades.

**4** Repeat 5–6 times.

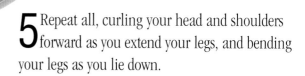

**5** Repeat all, curling your head and shoulders forward as you extend your legs, and bending your legs as you lie down.

**6** Repeat all, maintaining a curled Chest Lift position – moving your legs only.

# CO-ORDINATION

**1** Start as you did for Double Leg Stretch.

**2** As you exhale, curl your head and shoulders forward maintaining your legs at tabletop. Keep a strong centre, neutral pelvis and flat shoulder blades.

**3** Inhale as you stretch your legs up in front of you.

**4** Exhale, separate your legs into the stretchband and draw them together again.

**5** Inhale. Bend your knees and lie down with control.

**6** Repeat 5–10 times.

## NOTE
Apart from co-ordinating controlled movement and breathing, it is essential that you do not move your spine and pelvis when you separate your feet and legs. This is a challenge of your pelvic stability when your legs go in separate directions.

# Scapula Stability & Back Extension

***Purpose:*** *To strengthen your shoulder and middle upper back muscles for better posture. These exercises must not cause strain to your lower back and neck.*

## Back Extension With Arms

**1** Lie face down with your arms bent at a 90 degree angle next to your shoulders. Hold the stretchband loosely in your hands. Your pubic bone and lowest ribs should be anchored to the floor – make them your anchor points. Gently draw your shoulders back and hover your head and shoulders away from the floor, just enough to feel your middle upper back muscles engage. Zip your abdominals from pubic bone to navel, shrinking your stomach up to your spine, without moving your spine.

**2** As you balance on your anchor points, exhale stretching the stretchband and lightly grazing your little fingers along the floor. Keeping your stomach up and your shoulders back is important. Try to relax your neck.

**3** Inhale as you allow the stretchband to retract, ensuring that you maintain upper back and abdominal strength. Don't go round shouldered and don't be tempted to lift your back too high.

**4** Repeat 3–4 times before relaxing to the floor. Execute 3 sets in total.

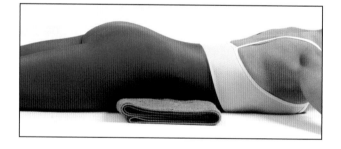

## Note
This exercise focuses on the muscles of your upper back and shoulders to prepare you for more advanced Pilates back strengthening. Try to resist shrugging, rounding or squeezing your shoulder blades together. If you feel your lower back overworking, you are possibly lifting too high or not lifting your abdominal muscles. You may need to place a folded towel under your abdomen to help support your spine.

# BREASTSTROKE

**1** Start as you did for Back Extension With Arms. The same principles apply throughout this exercise. The difference is that you start with your arms further forward on the floor. Maintain your abdominals and draw your shoulders back to feel your middle upper back engage. Anchor your ribs to the floor as you lift your chest slightly. Breathe in.

**2** As you exhale, stretch the stretchband so that your arms reach wide and arch your upper back further from the floor. Remember that you are bending from your upper back, not lower. Keep your arms slightly rotated so that the palms of your hands almost face each other.

**3** Inhale. Allow the stretchband to retract and slowly return your chest to the floor with your arms moving forward again.

**4** Repeat 5–6 times. Also try reverse breathing to challenge your muscle control.

## NOTE
Don't crane your neck to look up – imagine lengthening the area from the back of your ears to the top of your head. Keep your knuckles hovering lightly along the floor, keeping a sensation of opening your chest, while you shrink your abdominals up.

# SIDE STABILITY & HIP STRENGTH

*Purpose:* To challenge your balance and strengthen your stomach, back and hip muscles. Developing the ability to move your leg without moving your pelvis and spine requires co-ordination and causes your stabiliser muscles to work hard.

## LEG PRESS

**1** Lie on your side with your underneath leg slightly bent for better balance. Place the foot of your top leg inside the stretchband and hold the ends of the stretchband in one hand, next to your hip. Brace your abdominals as though they were a corset holding you together. Take care not to rotate your spine.

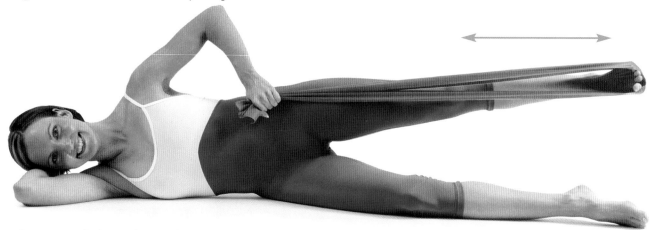

**2** As you exhale, push your foot into the stretchband and lengthen your leg away, in line with your body. You may aim your foot slightly behind your body in an effort to feel your gluteal muscles (the back of your hip) more. Do not arch your back.

**3** Inhale, allow the stretchband to loosen and your knee to bend. Keep your knee at hip height so you don't go knock-kneed.

**4** Repeat 6–10 times each side.

### NOTE
Balance on the underneath hip rather than your thigh and keep lengthening your top hip down towards your foot (even as your knee bends). Visualise the movement as being similar to propelling yourself off the side wall of a pool and through the water, using your hip and thigh muscles to achieve a straight and streamlined body. Scoop your abdominals constantly.

# SMALL CIRCLES

**1** Stay on your side as you were for Leg Press. Keep your top leg stretched straight with your foot in the stretchband. Emphasise the lengthening of your top hip towards your heel constantly and balance on your underneath hip rather than your thigh and scoop your abdominal muscles.

**2** Breathe calmly as you execute fast, small circles with your top leg. Maintain your leg at hip height and try not to let the circles go too far forward or backwards. They must be compact and your pelvis and spine must stay as still and strong as possible.

**3** Repeat approximately 10 circles in each direction, on each side.

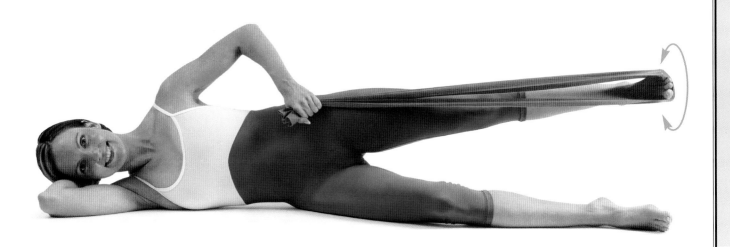

# SHOULDER & ARMWORK

***Purpose:*** *To strengthen your shoulder, arm, chest and upper back muscles for general strength and better posture.*

## NOTE

If you suffer from acute neck problems, some of this armwork may overuse muscles that are already tight and associated with your pain. Seek professional advice regarding appropriate neck stretches and postural strengthening exercises suitable for you.

## SHOULDER STRETCH

**1** Sit up, cross-legged, and hold the stretchband as though it was a pole. Lengthen your waist and ensure you are sitting on your sitting bones. Relax your neck and shoulders, pull your stomach to your spine and breathe normally.

**2** Keep your arms relatively straight and raise them to the ceiling. Your primary focus should be on good posture and allowing your shoulders to drop away from your ears. Be careful not to arch your back in order to raise your arms higher.

**3** Once your arms are up, allow them to move slightly further behind you to stretch your shoulder muscles. Breathe normally and hold momentarily before returning your arms down in front of you.

**4** Repeat 2–3 times.

## NOTE

For all sitting exercises over the next few chapters, your lower back must be comfortable. Please sit on a couple of phone books or a chair if it helps you to sit straighter.

# Rotator Cuff

**1** Sit tall, holding the stretchband with your hands about shoulder width apart. Lengthen up through your waist and pull your shoulders back, without arching your back.

**2** Exhale, rotating both shoulder joints as though they were hinges opening at the front. Don't necessarily squeeze your elbows against your body, but keep your upper arms completely vertical throughout the exercise. Keep a sense of your chest being open.

**3** Inhale. Relax but keep a good shoulder position.

**4** Repeat 10–12 times at a steady pace.

## Note

Keep a strong wrist position, thumbs on top of the stretchband with the back of your hands facing outward. You should feel the muscles at the back of your shoulder more than those at the front.

# RHOMBOIDS

**1** Sit tall, holding the stretchband looser now. Face the palms of your hands up.

**2** As you exhale lengthen your arms as though you are presenting a long platter to someone. Keep your elbows slightly bent, your shoulders back, your abdominals lifted and your neck relaxed.

**3** Inhale, relaxing your arms but keep your back and stomach strong.

**4** Repeat 10–12 times.

## MODIFICATION

If you are finding it difficult to eliminate neck tension, try wrapping the stretchband around your upper back and under your armpits. Stretch your arms in a similar manner. Emphasise your abdominals lengthening and visualise yourself leaning flat against a wall.

# SHOULDER & ARMWORK *(continued)*

## OFFERING

**1** Sit on the middle of the stretchband and hold the ends in your hands so that your thumbs point up during the exercise. Lengthen your spine and stabilise your shoulder blades.

**2** As you exhale, pull your arms up at an angle slightly wider than your knees. Maintain a very strong torso, keeping the tension out of your neck as much as possible. Do not hitch your shoulders up in effort to raise your arms.

**3** Inhale and relax, but don't slouch.

**4** Repeat 6–10 times.

# TRICEPS

**1** Sit tall and hold the stretchband in one hand. Dangle it over your shoulder and catch it behind you with the other hand, anchoring it to your seat. Keep your high elbow pointing forward and your shoulders square to your front. Relax your neck and be careful not to arch your back.

**2** As you exhale, raise your hand towards the ceiling maintaining the position of your upper arm. Ensure you don't hitch your shoulder up in effort to raise your hand.

**3** Inhale and control your arm, bending again to challenge muscle control.

**4** Repeat 10–12 times each arm.

# SHOULDER & ARMWORK *(continued)*

## TRICEPS EXTENDING

**1** Sit with your legs together in front of you. Lean your body forward towards your thighs without slouching. Keep your stomach lifted and relax your neck, drawing your shoulders back. Sit on the stretchband, hold the ends and reach both arms out behind you, shoulder width apart.

**2** As you exhale, lift your arms up behind you. Don't squeeze your shoulder blades together or go round shouldered. Keep scooping up your abdominals.

**3** Inhale as you lower your arms again.

**4** Repeat 10 times.

**5** With calm breathing, pulse your arms up and down with short quick movements at the height of your shoulder range.

**6** Repeat for 10–20 pulses.

**7** Hold your arms as high as you can, without being round shouldered and bend and stretch your elbows for further tricep work.

**8** Repeat 10 final extensions.

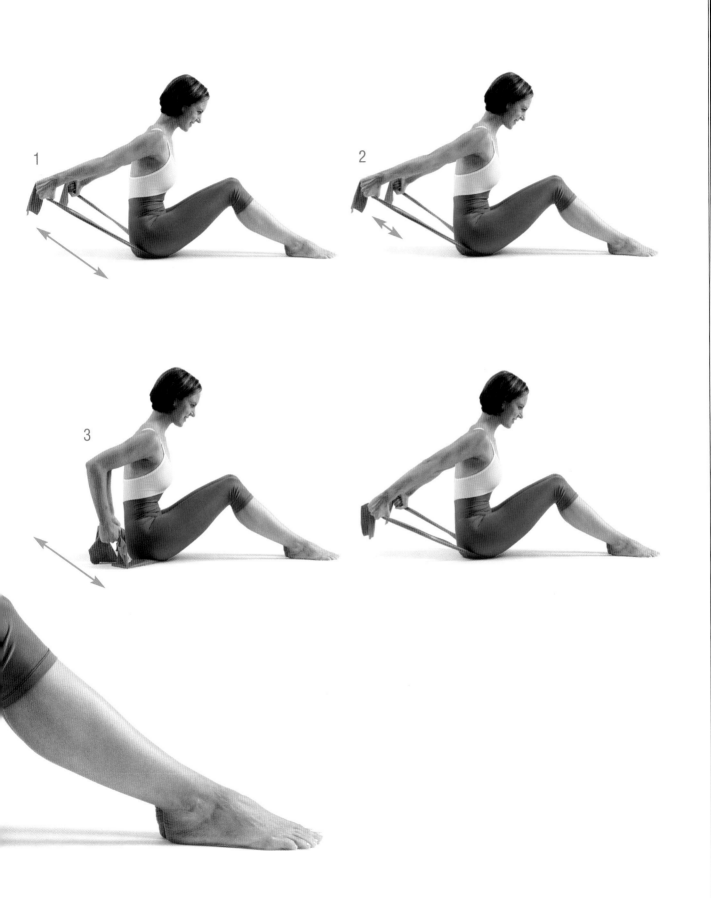

# FULL-BODY INTEGRATION

***Purpose:*** *To ultimately challenge your ability to have a whole-body focus while executing exercises that require stability of one part and movement of another. Often in Pilates you must feel opposing forces of resistance created by your own muscle effort in order to elongate, stabilise and move fluidly.*

## ROWING PREP (CHEST EXPANSION)

**1** Sit upright with your legs straight in front of you (bent if you need to be able to sit taller without lower back strain). Place the stretchband around the balls of your feet and hold the ends with your hands. Lengthen your waist with strong, taut abdominals and lightly pull your shoulders back.

**2** As you exhale, pull the stretchband and bend your arms next to your torso. Feel the breadth across your chest as your elbows reach back. Be careful not to lean backwards or use your neck.

**3** Inhale as you release the band. Keep your abdominals lifted.

**4** Repeat 10 times.

# ROWING PREP (BUTTERFLY)

**1** Sit as you were for Chest Expansion and hold the stretchband from beneath. You may have to lean forward a little and bend your knees.

**2** As you exhale, pull your arms wide – only as far as you feel the muscles at the back of your shoulders, not your neck. Keep your stomach and upper back lengthened and strong.

**3** Inhale as you release the band tension, but be careful not to slouch.

**4** Repeat 5–10 times.

# FULL BODY INTEGRATION *(continued)*

## SPINAL ROTATION (ARCHERY)

**1** Sit as you were for Rowing Prep with the stretchband around both feet.

**2** Exhale as you pull one end of the stretchband and rotate your upper torso to that side. Keep your pelvis and legs still and use your oblique abdominals, together with the muscles of your upper back, to control the twist.

**3** Inhale as you return to the front. Keep lengthening your abdominals and open your chest.

**4** Repeat, alternating sides up to 10 times.

# SPINAL ROTATION (SPINE TWIST)

**1** Sit tall with both legs together and bent in front of you. Wrap the stretchband around your upper back and under your armpits. Hold on to the ends and stretch your arms to the sides. Maintain a lengthened spine and good shoulder position throughout.

**2** As you exhale, rotate your upper torso with a double pulse action to one side.

**3** Inhale, returning to the centre. Maintain a long waist.

**4** Repeat, alternating sides for up to 10 times.

## NOTE
Once you have stretched your arms to the sides, try to keep your shoulders and arms still with good posture throughout the exercise. The movement comes from your waist and middle-lower thoracic spine.

# FULL BODY INTEGRATION *(continued)*

# Roll Back With Rotation

**1** Sit as you did for Spine Twist, with your legs bent and slightly apart. Hold the stretchband in your hands, palms up, just wider than shoulder width. Keep some tension on the stretchband so that you are aware of your shoulder and upper back muscles. Scoop up through your abdominal muscles. Inhale.

**2** As you exhale, pull your stomach to your spine and roll back to the point where you feel moderate challenge with your abdominals. Inhale. Hold still and continue to keep some tension on the stretchband.

**3** Exhale. Rotate your upper body without losing your deep abdominal work. Keep your pelvis and legs still. Inhale as you return to the centre, maintaining a stable pelvis and the same amount of roundness through the spine.

**4** Exhale. Rotate to the other side. Inhale. Return to the centre.

**5** Exhale. Roll forward towards your legs and sit tall.

**6** Repeat 4–5 times.

# STRETCHES

***Purpose:*** *To release and elongate muscles that have been under tension or performing strength work. Combining strength, mobility and flexibility aspects to your exercise regime will promote a balanced physique.*

## THORACIC RELEASE

**1** Sit upright with your legs shoulder width apart, or slightly wider. If you are unable to sit tall with your legs straight, either bend your knees or sit on a couple of books. Lengthen your waist and abdominal muscles and breathe normally.

**2** Place both hands on one leg and as you exhale, roll head-first towards your leg and slide your hands towards your shin. Ease into the stretch, relaxing both shoulders towards the floor. Try to keep the opposite hip anchored to the floor.

**3** You may hold the stretch for 2–3 full breaths, then engage your deep abdominals as you roll up, lengthening your waist upright initially and rebuilding the spine piece-by-piece until you sit tall.

**4** Repeat 4–6 times in total, alternating sides.

# Psoas Stretch (Supine)

**1** Lying on your back, place a cushion or rolled towel under the lowest part of your hips so that your lower back can still relax towards the floor. Hold one thigh up to the side of your chest, aiming for your shoulder. Lengthen your other leg along the floor.

**2** Breathe normally and relax for 20–30 seconds.

**3** Repeat on your other leg and repeat both again if the stretch feels beneficial for the front of your outstretched thigh and hip.

## NOTE
The cushion or towel is optional, but will ensure a deeper hip flexor stretch.

# STRETCHES *(continued)*

## PSOAS STRETCH (KNEELING)

**1** Kneel on one knee and lunge forward so that your weight is on your front heel and both hands. Ensure that both knees align with your shoulders so you don't go knock-kneed, and allow your back leg to relax so you feel the front of that hip stretching.

**2** Hold for 20–30 seconds.

**3** Repeat on your other leg and again on both legs.

# Neck Stretch

**1** Sit upright. Keep your shoulders back and carefully tilt your head to one side – ear-to-shoulder – without allowing your shoulders to raise. You may need to stand in front of a mirror to see if you are keeping your shoulders level and that you are not rotating your neck and head.

**2** Hold momentarily and repeat on the other side.

**3** Repeat both sides.

# POWER PILATES

## WORKOUT SEQUENCE

**CENTRING & BREATHING**
1 SCAPULA MOVEMENT
x 5

**POSTURE AWARENESS**
2 ARM OPENINGS
x 5

**WARM UP**
3 PELVIC CURL
x 4

**WARM UP**
4 CHEST LIFT
x 5

**WARM UP**
5 FOOTWORK
x 10 + 10 toes only

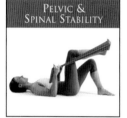
**PELVIC & SPINAL STABILITY**
6 BEND & STRETCH
x 6 each leg

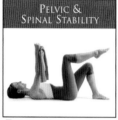
**PELVIC & SPINAL STABILITY**
7 DEAD BUG
x 6 each leg

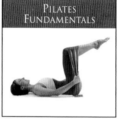
**PILATES FUNDAMENTALS**
8 HUNDRED
10 full breaths

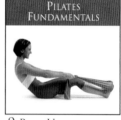
**PILATES FUNDAMENTALS**
9 ROLL UP
x 4 - 6

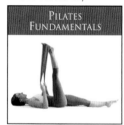
**PILATES FUNDAMENTALS**
10 LEG CIRCLES
x 6 each way, each leg

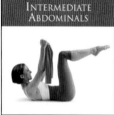
**INTERMEDIATE ABDOMINALS**
11 SINGLE LEG STRETCH
x 6

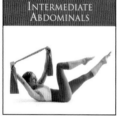
**INTERMEDIATE ABDOMINALS**
12 CRISS-CROSS
x 6

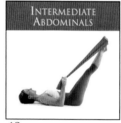
**INTERMEDIATE ABDOMINALS**
13 DOUBLE LEG STRETCH x 10

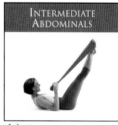
**INTERMEDIATE ABDOMINALS**
14 CO-ORDINATION
x 5

**SCAPULA STABILITY & BACK EXTENSION**
15 BACK EXTENSION WITH ARMS x 3

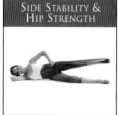
**SIDE STABILITY & HIP STRENGTH**
16 SMALL CIRCLES
x 10 each way, each leg

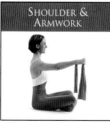
**SHOULDER & ARMWORK**
17 SHOULDER STRETCH
x 4

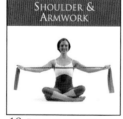
**SHOULDER & ARMWORK**
18 RHOMOIDS x 10

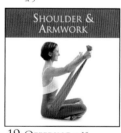
**SHOULDER & ARMWORK**
19 OFFERING x 10

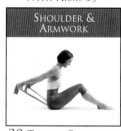
**SHOULDER & ARMWORK**
20 TRICEPS EXTENDING
x 20 pulses + 10 extensions

**FULL BODY INTEGRATION**
21 ROWING PREP
(CHEST EXPANSION)
x 10

**FULL BODY INTEGRATION**
22 ROWING PREP
(BUTTERFLY) x 6

**FULL BODY INTEGRATION**
23 SPINAL ROTATION
(ARCHERY) x 6

**FULL BODY INTEGRATION**
24 ROLL BACK WITH ROTATION x 4

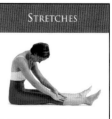
**STRETCHES**
25 COMPLETE ALL STRETCHES
(Pages 186–189)

# Glossary

**ABDOMINAL MUSCLES**
There are four layers of abdominal muscles. The six-pack crunches you forward; external and internal obliques (waist muscles) rotate and twist the torso with the internal obliques also assisting in trunk stabilisation; and the deeper layer (transversus abdominus) acts to stabilise the spine against any of these movements once the spine and pelvis is stable in a certain position. Transversus is often referred to as one of the core stabilisers.

**GLUTEALS**
The glutes are the muscle group of the buttocks, which contribute to hip movement and stabilisation of the pelvis and lower back.

**HAMSTRINGS**
The group of muscles at the back of the thigh which originate at the sitting bone and insert at the back of the knee. These help move the thigh backwards and/or bend the knee.

**HIP FLEXORS**
Muscles at the front of the hip (groin area), one of which is the psoas. They contract to lift the thigh to the torso. The psoas directly affect the lower back if tight and/or weak.

**LATS (LATISSIMUS DORSI)**
Large muscle of the back which engages as the arm draws backwards.

**PECS (PECTORALIS MINOR/MAJOR)**
Muscles of the chest and front of the shoulder which are commonly tight due to the amount of activity we do with the arms in front of our torsos, such as lifting objects.

**PELVIC FLOOR**
Thin layer of muscles suspended across the pelvic girdle which supports the weight of the abdominal organs and shares nerve connections with both deep abdominal muscles and the respiratory diaphragm. Activation of the pelvic floor contributes to strengthening of the abdominal region.

**RHOMBOIDS**
Muscles between the thoracic spine and the shoulder blades which contribute to scapula stabilisation for better posture.

**ROTATOR CUFF**
Four muscles comprise the rotator cuff which act synergistically to hold the shoulder joint stable and aligned.

**SCAPULA (SCAPULAE – PLURAL)**
The shoulder blade, which helps make up the shoulder joint, provides attachments for many of the upper back muscles. Stabilising the scapulae flat against the ribcage is essential for good posture.

**SITTING BONES**
These are the lowest boney protrusions of the pelvis that you are aware of when you sit on a hard surface. They provide an attachment site for the hamstrings, and when you sit exactly on them, or slightly behind them, you are usually in a neutral pelvic alignment.

**SPINE**
The spine is made up of different sections. The cervical spine is that of the neck; thoracic being the middle upper back and the attachment for all the ribs; the lumbar spine is that of the lower back; and the saccral and coccygeal are that of the pelvis and tailbone.

**SUPINE**
This is the anatomical term for lying on your back. Prone is when you are lying face down.

**TRICEPS**
These muscles are those of the back of the upper arm, running from the back of the shoulder to the elbow.

# CONCLUSION

Joseph Pilates is considered to have been ahead of his time in his strategies for full-body strengthening and his analysis of overall healthy living. It is said that he continued to define, refine and challenge his philosophy of body conditioning throughout his years, endeavouring to assist individuals in overcoming physical limitations. Now, as modern physical science continues to discover more about how our muscles and joints move, Pilates Masters continue to evolve the movement which is based on Joseph's original teachings. However, the principles behind the movement will always remain the same and will continue to have great impact on the health and lives of those who practise Pilates.

Incorporating a stretchband into a Pilates workout creates a new dimension for you to enhance your experience with the Method. As you adopt routine Pilates practice into your life, you will discover a centredness and greater ease of movement. It is always important that you periodically return to the basics in order to understand how the fundamental principles completely affect the continuing benefits you will gain from this unique method of full-body conditioning.

## ABOUT THE AUTHOR

Jennifer Pohlman was first introduced to Pilates as a dance student while completing a Bachelor of Dance degree at the Victorian College of the Arts in Melbourne. She later trained as an instructor and taught the Pilates Method in Brisbane and Gold Coast studios before establishing her own Gold Coast studio, called Pilates InsideOut. Her approach to the Pilates Method is both dynamic and innovative and she is experienced with clients of all fitness levels and ages – from athletes to clinical rehabilitation patients.